the jewish princess cookbook

having your cake & eating it...

Georgie Tarn & Tracey Fine

quadrille

First published in 2006 by
Quadrille Publishing Limited
Alhambra House
27-31 Charing Cross Road
London WC2H 0LS

Reprinted in 2007
10 9 8 7 6 5 4 3 2

Text © 2006 Georgie Tarn & Tracey Fine
Illustrations © 2006 Karen Greenberg
Design and layout © 2006 Quadrille Publishing Limited

editorial director Jane O'Shea
project editor Jamie Ambrose
designer Claire Peters
production Funsho Asemota

Cataloguing in Publication Data: a catalogue record for this book is available
from the British Library.

ISBN: 978 184400 362 4

Printed and bound in China

dedication

This book is dedicated to our grandmothers, who are truly loved and missed. They always had the luxury of time when it came to their grandchildren. They inspired us to cook delicious food. They never worried about their waistlines (this made us worry about ours). They always had an opinion on everything: even if they were wrong, they were right. They handed down to us a wonderful sense of *Yiddishkeit*. They gave us heartfelt cuddles within their enormous, non-surgically enhanced breasts. They made our families' lives more colourful with their ability to start *broygeses*.

To Grandma Kitty and Nana Lily.
We are sure you are *shlepping naches*
from up above!

contents

acknowledgements

As I'll explain in a minute, this book grew out of a midlife crisis. I have to say that Tracey and I found this crisis great fun, complete with loads of hysterical telephone conversations and jumping up and down outside very posh offices in the West End (certainly recapturing our youth – circa age 11). Through all the excitement I actually lost loads of weight without even having to sniff the gym – bloody marvellous! So as I sit here thinking about my midlife crisis, my advice would be that if you are contemplating one of your own, and you are a Jewish Princess, just make sure it's one that is PPP: Positive, Productive, and of course, Princess-like.

Now, on to the business at hand, which is thanking people.

We are surrounded by incredible friends. I say 'incredible', not only because they seem to know everyone in the world, but also because of how unselfish and generous they have all been with their advice. It really has been a revelation that all my friends' husbands and boyfriends are actually incredibly knowledgeable, professional and *clever*, because when we go out and about, visit the latest restaurants, etc., etc., you only think of them as *Husbands* or *Boyfriends* (need I say more?). You never think of them heading up boardroom meetings or taking on their own global, midlife crises. They are just people you love and adore, take the mickey out of and have a great time with.

We would like to thank our mothers, Sandra Chester and Helen Fine (yes, you can now tell your friends); our fathers, David Chester and Tony Fine, who always answer emergency JP phone calls, even on the golf-course; and inlaws Bobbie and Irvin Tarn, whose toilet stop has proved invaluable on the way up to those West End meetings. We would, of course, like to thank Georgie's husband, RAT, and Tracey's partner, Richard de Smith, who have been our 'rocks'; our children, Cassie, Eden, Darcy, Max and Channie, whose talents have contributed to this work;

and our brothers and sisters, nieces and nephews, who have enjoyed sampling The Ultimate Friday Night Dinners again and again and again.

Then there's Anne Marie Owens (The Hairdresser), who knew Dorie Simmonds (The Agent), who knew Quadrille (The Publisher), where we met the wonderful Jane O'Shea. Thanks, too, to Stephen Marks, for all the phone calls regarding net and gross – yes, we've finally got it ('gross you get, net you vet'); Paul Taylor, for slotting us in between his high-powered business meetings; Roger Law, for meeting us for a cup of tea, a slice of cake and inspirational advice; William Miller, for your time and patience; and Ray Simone, for believing in us.

And thank you Mel Goldberg (you were there from the start); Andrew Thompson, our lawyer (who didn't have a clue what he was taking on); and Debbie Jones, our bank manager (we love you – you gave us a credit card!). We would like to thank our most understanding editor, Jamie Ambrose, who has been in intensive JP training; designer Claire Peters; PR (Princess Relations) people Clare Lattin and Emily Sanders; and all at Quadrille for making our Princess wish come true.

Finally, big thanks to the Jewish Princesses: Karen Gerrard, Elaine Grant, Zilda Collins, Lisa Marks, Sima Fine, Deborah Bright, Mandy Stanley, Auntie Rosalind Chester, Sharon Payne, Michelle Grossman and Sylvia de Smith for parting with their precious family recipes, and last but not least, Andrea (Princess G's au pair).

1

introduction

princess philosophy

I'm proud to admit that I am a Jewish Princess. I believe that every woman has a little bit of a JP in her – or if she doesn't, then she certainly should.

So just what *is* a Jewish Princess, I hear you ask? Well, the usual stereotype seems to be 'spoilt little rich girl who spends all her days shopping and beautifying herself' – let me tell you, that is simply untrue and quite unfair. After all, I never spend *all* day shopping and beautifying myself! I just like to enjoy life, and part of the enjoyment of life is food and feeding your family.

Do I love cooking? 'Not particularly' is the answer to that, so why write a cookbook? Well, as I approached my fortieth birthday, I realized that I was having a midlife crisis – but of course, being a Jewish Princess, mine was taking a rather different turn. I wouldn't contemplate an affair, and I certainly wasn't going to have a nervous breakdown or cut off all my hair (heaven forbid!). No, my crisis was going to be *productive*, and as I seem to have inherited the good-cook gene from my mother (who now no longer cooks, but can be found somewhere in a Floridian mall) and my grandmother-over-sholom (a Jewish expression for when we speak of the passed-over – not Passover: that's a Jewish holiday), a cookbook seemed like the most natural thing to do. I mean, we all have to eat, and even Jewish Princesses can't go out to eat *every* night.

And if I have to do something, I like to do it well, even if it's not exactly at the top of my 'Have to Do' list (which, by the way, is always *very* long).

So when the idea of *The Jewish Princess Cookbook* came to me, I immediately thought of my friends – after all, who can you share all the memories with? I phoned my oldest and most Princess-like friend, Tracey, to ask her what she thought of the idea and whether she wanted to be involved. She considered it for about half a second and jumped aboard.

The first thing we did was to delegate our jobs on the book: I made lunch; she made the cake.

the power of food

Food and eating lie at the very centre of Jewish culture. I really think the Old Testament was our first menu – the festivals give us such wonderful delicacies. When I think of Chanukah, I think of doughnuts. The Jewish New Year? Honey cake. And so it goes on and on.

Just think of your favourite cake. Or, if you're not a 'cake' person (*I* certainly don't know who you are, but maybe you're out there...) think of your favourite food. How does it make you feel?

When someone takes the time and trouble to make your favourite food, how do you feel about them?

Grateful. *Happy.*

Now, when people are grateful and *happy*, they are in your power. So forget the power of speech, the power of song, the power of the written word; let's get down to basics and realize that with a few eggs, some flour and a good chunk of chocolate we have the power of making others *happy*. And happiness leads to a loving home, a loving partner – and of course, lovely *things*.

It really is true that the way to a Jewish man's heart is through his stomach. If you asked Jewish men whether they would prefer a nice bowl of chicken soup or a romp upstairs, I'll bet eight out of ten of them would go for the chicken soup – especially if it contained matzo balls.

Yet the Jewish Princess of today isn't like her mother or grandmother; she's not going to be a slave to the house or the kitchen. Today's Jewish Princess wants to run a wonderful home, look good, produce lovely food, look good, look after her children – did I mention 'look good'? Sure, we want to have our cake and eat it, but we also want to look as if we haven't!

In order to do this, we have to have some tricks up our sleeves. While I have no objection to cheating in this area, and will admit sometimes to using convenience food and doctoring it to make it look like my own (oh, come *on* – we've all done it!), there truly is nothing like the satisfaction of producing wonderful homemade food.

Well, OK, there are many other satisfying things, such as 1) shopping, 2) shopping, and 3) shopping.

But I digress.

In order to have a very, very satisfying life, then, use *The Jewish Princess Cookbook* to produce food that is 1) easy, 2) non-time-consuming and 3) has fewer than ten ingredients, on average, per recipe. Oh – and of course tastes delicious and looks incredibly difficult.

If *I* can do it, *you* can do it!

So take back your take-outs, stock up your larders, forward plan, try a little bit of imagination, and use this book. You will then have the power of food in your hands.

the pay-off

The power of food produces many valuable dividends. Respect and adoration are just two of these, and when you see your friends and family loving your food, it really does give you a feeling of immense satisfaction – especially when they think you've been slaving over a hot stove, and you haven't (but no need to correct them there).

The recipes you will find in *The Jewish Princess Cookbook* are simple, easy to follow and have a fantastic success rate – but don't feel you have to be a slave to them. Whenever you cook, always think of the flavours you like and be creative. Use recipes, including the ones in this book, as guides, but if you fancy adding something or giving the recipe a twist, try it. You never know what fantastic new thing you may discover.

Always remember: it's not only the food, but how you present it that earns the seal of approval from your friends and family. So go on: take the plunge. I'm sure you will still have time left over for all those other, more satisfying, and very important things.

Which reminds me...

Got to go now – hairdresser's appointment!

jewish dietary rules
or, the kosher noshtra

Contrary to popular belief, the rules that govern the Jewish diet are *not*:

* EAT, EAT, EAT, or
* have a little (or a lot) of what you fancy, or
* when you entertain, always make sure there is enough food
  in case your guests bring ten friends with them.

No, the Jewish dietary rules date back to the Old Testament (a best-seller.) In this book, the Jewish people were given strict rules that applied to every aspect of eating – partly because, you know, even in those days, Jewish Princesses were thinking about that four-letter word: *diet*.

If you thought the Atkins was tricky, or found the G.I. Diet a little difficult to follow, or decided that the Blood Group Diet was far too complicated (especially if you don't know your blood group), then let me put all this in perspective. These are nothing – NOTHING – compared to following the 'K Diet', otherwise known as keeping kosher.

The Jewish kosher diet puts all others in the shade. It's complicated, you're on it for a lifetime, and sometimes it is very tempting to fall off the wagon. As far as the latter is concerned, it is up to every Jewish Princess to decide how disciplined she is prepared to be, but for anyone else who wants to try it, here are the highlights.

kosher meat

When it comes to meat, to follow the kosher diet you must only choose from animals that chew the cud and have split hooves – so beef and lamb are in and pork, camel and horse are out. Which is fine with me; I personally would never dream of eating Black Beauty (or a camel).

Not only are certain animals forbidden, but certain cuts of meat must also be avoided. However, if you buy your meat at a kosher butcher, you will never go wrong, as I can assure you they are very strict about the kinds and cuts of meat which are stocked on their shelves.

Fish are a little more straightforward. You can eat all fish which have scales and fins, but all types of shellfish are not permitted.

treif and parev

All unkosher food is known as *treif*, which actually means 'torn.' This does not mean torn between choosing Parma ham or just having the melon; it means you're not allowed to eat flesh that has been torn from one animal by another animal. All animals killed in this manner are forbidden.

Also, milk and meat must not be eaten together at the same meal, so no hamburgers – or should I say beefburgers? – with milkshakes.

Foods that contain neither milk nor meat are known as *parev*. This means these foods can be eaten with either meat or dairy meals – for example, fish, fruit, vegetables and non-animal, manufactured food products, such as non-dairy creamers.

If this all sounds like a lot of palaver, there is a bright side. For every Jewish Princess, keeping a kosher home means the added bonus of being able to indulge in buying not one, but at least *two* sets of crockery, cutlery, saucepans and linen, in order to keep all those milky and meaty dishes separate. Of course, you should never need an excuse to hit the housewares department of your favourite store, but this at least validates the urge.

As you can see, the basis of a kosher diet is something that requires discipline and willpower. Luckily for you, I've already done the hard work of making sure that all the recipes in this book are kosher.

For all Jewish Princesses who make the decision to follow this way of eating, I just want to say:

Mazel tov! You're following the oldest diet in the book.

What does a Jewish Princess
make for dinner?

Reservations!

a word about life

Now before you start trying the recipes, I want to share with you a very important part of JP philosophy. You might not catch on immediately, but bear with me, please, and read on to the end. There's plenty of time for cooking afterward.

I love Champagne, especially Princess Pink Champagne (naturally). I love the bottle: curvaceous and crowned with gold. A dry *pop!* The cork is released, and there's the slow descent of the liquid into a tall, slim glass. The colour is unique: like liquid candlelight. This perfect drink is to be sipped and savoured, and it reminds me of all the good times in my life.

Except, actually, the first time I ever drank it.

I was 16 years old, out on a date and dressed to kill in a new lilac leather dress (well, it *was* the early '80s). I wanted to impress this boy-man sitting in front of me, and being a very sophisticated teenage Princess, I ordered a Champagne cocktail. Unfortunately, nerves and an empty stomach got the better of me, and I spent most of the evening in the ladies', trying to dry my leather belt which accidentally got flushed down the loo. This unfortunate incident did not cool my ardour for Champagne, however. I just left out the cocktail part after that and went for the pink stuff straight.

And here's where the philosophy bit comes in. You see, above all else, the Jewish Princess knows that life is for living – that's with a capital 'L'. This isn't a dress rehearsal, after all (though dresses do, of course, play a very important part in every Jewish Princess's life).

The first rule of being a JP is this: if there is an excuse to celebrate – like buying your first pair of Jimmy Choos, or even when (not if) the first recipe you try in this books works a treat – then bring on and bring out the Champagne. This cool, delicious beverage makes every occasion a celebration.

You could try it right now, just to get the hang of it. Fill your glass and toast: to life – *lechayim!*

the princess pledge

* I pledge to have a clean and tidy home (but I never said I would do the cleaning and tidying).

* I pledge to acknowledge and embrace my *mishegasses*, as they make me who I am.

* I pledge that I will be prepared to go on holiday, even at very, very short notice.

* I pledge to buy lots of evening shoes and make sure I wear them.

* I pledge to have the bling, but not to wear everything (at once).

* I pledge that if I find an item of clothing that really suits me, I will buy it in more than one colour.

* I pledge to give rather than receive (except when it comes to jewellery).

* I pledge that I will make the most of myself, embrace the good bits and visit the plastic surgeon for the bad bits.

* I pledge that when I visit public toilets, I will do the 'Princess Perch'.

* I pledge that I will respect my manicurist, hairdresser and beautician, for they are in the background, allowing me to step into the foreground.

* I pledge to treasure my true friends, as they are the diamonds that every girl needs.

* I swear allegience to Gucci, Louis Vuitton, Prada, D&G, Dior, Missoni, DKNY, Chanel, Yves Saint Laurent, Fendi, Mui Mui, Mark Jacobs, Tod's, Jimmy Choo, Etro, Moschino, Calvin Klein, Hermès, Lanvin, Givenchy, Thierry Mugler, Roberto Cavalli, Marni, Georgio Armani, La Perla, Juicy Couture, Seven Jeans, Citizens of Humanity, Escada, Bottega Veneta, Alexander McQueen, Versace, Vivien Westwood, Diane von Furstenberg, Stella McCartney, Burberry, Emanuel Ungaro, Ralph Lauren, Chloé, Valentino, Graff, Cartier, Kauffman de Suisse, Tiffany, Asprey, Rolex, Chopard, Van Cleef & Arples, David Morris, Boodles and Bvlgari. I apologize to any I've missed, but I'm sure I'll be visiting your store soon!

2

appetizers

appetizer surprisers

I really look forward to visiting a new, trendy, 'spendy' type of restaurant. All too often, however, we end up at a 'Once-r': the restaurant you visit only once because the service and food are so bad and the prices so high that you'd never dream of going back for 'seconds'. It generally happens this way:

As I take in the beautiful surroundings, I hope the menu will arrive promptly so I can savour my glass of the pink stuff. Eventually the waiter notices me (the one at the centre table, gesticulating wildly) and we order – well, *I* order, as Hubby seems to think I'll somehow magically know what he wants. At this point I have to resort to sign language, either because the waiter doesn't speak a word of English, or because the restaurant is so noisy (due to designer stone floors, stainless-steel walls and chattering people) that normal speech is impossible.

Then The Wait begins – and so does my sense of Food Foreboding. I've ordered a *hot* appetizer, and seeing as the encounter with the waiter hasn't gone well, I'll be surprised if it's not lukewarm when my fork makes contact.

What is it with Once-r restaurants? They charge a fortune, yet make you wait an eternity before delivering anything. By the time the appetizer appears, you've already eaten a loaf of bread, a bowl of olives and nuts from the bar. Now, I usually find the appetizer the most enjoyable part of the meal. Why? Well, by the time I've finished the breadbasket, the olives and nuts, had words with the manager, and noshed my way through the first course, I'm simply too full and too exhausted to enjoy anything else.

After many such disastrous dinners I now really look forward to being entertained by friends or to entertaining them in my own home. Even though my abode may be a little last season, the chairs are comfy, the pink stuff is ready and waiting, and the food always arrives on time. I also know that when I serve appetizers (at the *correct* temperature), my guests will enjoy them, but they'll still have plenty of appetite left to relish the rest of their meal – and I *know* they'll be coming back for seconds!

pink grapefruit with brown sugar

serves *as many as you like!*

pink grapefruit
  (allow 1 per person)

dark brown sugar
  (2 teaspoons per person)

Peel the pink grapefruit, removing all of the pips and as much pith as possible.

Cut each into segments.

Place the segmented grapefruit into a frying pan and sprinkle with the sugar.

Cook briefly over a high heat – as the sugar melts, toss your grapefruit segments so that the fruit is well-coated. This whole process takes less than two minutes, so you could say ready in a jiffy – or should I say a Jaffa?

Serve in individual glass dishes.

This is a delicious, easy starter, warm and sweet on the outside and cool and zingy on the inside.

melon balls in champagne

serves 6

1 cantaloup melon
1 honeydew melon
about 175ml champagne, or
   other white sparkling wine

4 tablespoons runny honey
whites of 2 medium eggs, beaten
110g caster sugar

Ball both melons and mix the pieces into a bowl.

Mix the Champagne and honey, then pour over the melon balls.

Chill.

Take some Champagne glasses and dip the rim of each into the beaten egg-white, then into the caster sugar.

Spoon the melon mixture into the glasses, making sure there is plenty of liquid in each glass.

Lechayim!

watermelon with feta

serves *as many as you like!*

1 watermelon (preferably
   seedless) – allow five small
   pieces per person
vodka
feta cheese, cubed – allow
   ten cubes per person

virgin olive oil
1 basil leaf per person,
   for decoration

Cut the watermelon into slices and remove the rind (and seeds, if there are any). Place the slices in the shape of a flower on each plate.

Drizzle a little vodka over the melon.

Place ten small cubes of feta cheese around the edge of each plate.

Drizzle a small amount of olive oil over the cheese.

Place a basil leaf in the middle of each plate for decoration.

A delicious, refreshing, quick and simple appetizer that looks wonderful. Jewish Princesses will love it!

chopped herring

serves 8

500g sweet herring fillets,
    with onion
2 eating apples, peeled
    and grated
2 medium hard-boiled eggs

6 digestive biscuits
1 tablespoon ground almonds
1 slice of white bread,
    crust removed
2 teaspoons caster sugar

Drain the herrings and pat dry with a kitchen towel.

Mix all of the ingredients in a food processor until smooth.

This is delicious served with toasted black bread and cream cheese.

easy salmon pâté

serves 6 as an appetizer, 4 for a girly lunch

275g (roughly 2 fillets) red
  salmon, skinned
275g (roughly 2 fillets) rainbow
  trout, skinned
1 bunch of dill
1 medium onion, peeled
2 lemons

salt and black pepper to taste
5 teaspoons creamed horseradish
1 heaped tablespoon sour cream
3 tablespoons low-fat
  natural yoghurt
175g smoked salmon, 'un-leaved'

Wash and place the salmon and rainbow trout fillets in a saucepan along with half the dill, the onion and the juice of one of the lemons. Season with salt and black pepper, then cover with water.

Bring the fillets to the boil and boil for one minute.

Turn off the heat (if you're using an electric hob, move the fish away) and place a lid on top. The fish will carry on cooking in the hot water.

After 30 minutes, remove the fillets from the saucepan and place in a bowl.

In a separate bowl, mix the horseradish, sour cream, yoghurt and the juice of half a lemon.

Add the rest of the dill, finely chopped (I use scissors), and some salt and pepper to season.

When the fillets are cool, add the creamed horseradish mixture and blend well until the mixture forms a smooth pâté. Refrigerate.

Take a piece of foil or greaseproof paper and place the smoked salmon on top. Season with black pepper and lemon juice.

Spoon the fish pâté onto the smoked salmon, leaving a gap at the bottom so that you can easily roll the salmon lengthwise over the pâté.

Fold the smoked salmon over the pâté, making a parcel in the shape of a tube.

Wrap the foil or greaseproof paper over the salmon so that it looks like a Christmas cracker, then refrigerate.

Before serving, remove the foil or paper and cut into slices. You can decorate it with thin slices of lemon, if desired.

This starter looks very impressive indeed – so give yourself a pâté on the back!

caramelized onion tomato and brie tart

serves 6

500g ready-to-roll frozen puff
   or shortcrust pastry
a sprinkling of plain flour
1 x 300g jar caramelized onions
1-2 punnets small, firm tomatoes
   (cherry tomatoes are great for this:
   they're sweet and look the biz!)

250g mild, creamy brie
dash of olive oil
salt and pepper to taste
fresh basil leaves (enough to
   scatter over the dish)

Preheat oven to 180°C/350°F/gas mark 4.

Roll out the pastry so that it is just large enough to fit a 28cm flan tin. Lay this in the tin.

Sprinkle plain flour lightly over the surface of the pastry, then spread a thin layer of caramelized onion over the top.

Halve the tomatoes and lay them around the pastry in rings, slightly overlapping, until you get to the centre. Cover all areas quite tightly, as the tomatoes will shrink when cooked.

Slice the brie thinly and dot it over the top of the tomatoes, leaving a 2.5cm gap between pieces as it will melt and spread sufficiently.

Sprinkle with a dash of olive oil, then add the salt, pepper and basil.

Bake in the preheated oven for 35 minutes. The pastry should be golden brown.

Serve warm or cold.

This simple dish looks spectacular. It's lovely for lunch.

The first Jewish Princess, Eve,
decided that her partner needed
to be put on a healthier regime.
So for starters he would have
to eat a piece of fruit a day.

Unfortunately, she chose the
wrong one.

roasted asparagus with lemon mayo

serves 4

2 tablespoons low-fat mayonnaise
2 tablespoons sour cream
juice of 1 lemon
  (divided into two portions)

rock salt and black pepper
2 large bunches of asparagus
extra-virgin olive oil

First, make the lemon mayonnaise. Combine the mayonnaise, sour cream, half the lemon juice, and salt and black pepper to taste. Refrigerate.

Preheat the oven to 200°C/400°F/gas mark 6.

Wash and trim the asparagus spears and place them in a non-stick roasting tin.

Drizzle them with the olive oil and the other half of the lemon juice. Turn the asparagus spears over so that they have a fine coating of the olive oil and lemon juice on both sides.

Season with black pepper and rock salt to taste.

Roast the asparagus for 20 minutes, turning the spears over halfway through cooking.

Take out of the oven and leave to cool. Once cold, refrigerate or serve straight away.

To serve, place the asparagus on a serving dish with the mayo on the side.

Delicious for dunking!

roasted red and yellow peppers

serves 6

7 red peppers
7 yellow peppers
1 x 150g (drained weight) tin
  pitted black olives
1 dessertspoon balsamic vinegar

olive oil to coat the peppers
  (infused with garlic or basil,
  if you prefer)
2 teaspoons caster sugar

Preheat the oven to 180°C/350°F/gas mark 4.

Slice the peppers into large chunks and deseed.

Rinse the olives and add them to the peppers.

Place in an ovenproof dish and pour on a good splash
of balsamic vinegar.

Add enough olive oil so that the peppers are covered.

Sprinkle the sugar over the top.

Mix the ingredients together with a spatula.

Bake in the preheated oven for one hour, turning the peppers
every 20 minutes so they do not burn, until the vegetables are soft.

*This dish can be served on its own, or for an appetizer you can
make some toasted French bread pieces and put the peppers on
top, along with a handful of basil. For a main course, just add a
handful of cherry tomatoes to the above. It also makes a delicious
pasta sauce.*

salmon fish cakes

serves 6

2 x 180g tins red salmon
  (it's easier to buy boneless)
1 large onion, grated
1 large egg, beaten

salt and black pepper to taste
50g medium matzo meal
corn oil, for frying
sea salt, for serving

Combine the salmon, grated onion and beaten egg. Add salt and pepper to taste, then add the matzo meal to bind the mixture.

Form the mixture into patties and fry in a wok or frying pan, using enough corn oil to cover. Fry until light brown.

Just before serving, grind a little sea salt over the fish cakes. They're extra-delicious if you serve them warm.

If you wish to give these a Thai-style twist, then add some chopped coriander and a little lemon-grass paste. Use kitchen paper to rest the fried fish cakes on, as this will remove any excess oil.

sesame chicken balls

serves 8 as an appetizer

500g chicken mince
4 teaspoons teriyaki marinade
3 tablespoons fine matzo meal
½ teaspoon caster sugar
2 medium eggs

half an onion, grated
salt and black pepper to taste
275g sesame seeds
vegetable oil, for frying

Mix together all the ingredients except the sesame seeds. Season well with black pepper, adding a little salt to taste.

Wet your hands and roll the mixture into little balls, then dip each into a bowl filled with the sesame seeds, covering the chicken mixture.

Fry in vegetable oil until cooked.

Serve with dipping sauce on the side (you can use a sweet chilli sauce or mango chutney), or serve with Chinese cabbage salad for a little bit of 'Ko-chin' – Kosher Chinese!

spinach bake (kugel)

serves 6 as a starter, or 4 for lunchtime with the girls

350g fine dry pasta
  (such as *lockshen* noodles)
350g spinach
25g unsalted butter

1 packet onion soup mix
350g mascarpone cheese
3 medium eggs
1 handful of pine nuts

Preheat the oven to 180°C/350°F/gas mark 4.

Boil the pasta according to instructions on the packet until it's *al dente*.

Put the spinach in a saucepan with the butter and gently fry until limp.

Combine the soup mix with the cheese and eggs. Add the cooked pasta and spinach and mix well.

Grease an ovenproof flan dish and fill with the mixture.

Sprinkle the pine nuts over the top.

Bake for an hour until crispy, or 15 minutes if cooking in individual greased ramekins.

Delicious served either hot or cold.

latkes (potato pancakes)

makes approximately 50 cocktail-sized

2.25 kilos maris piper or other
  good-quality potatoes
3 large onions
2 tablespoons self-raising flour

salt and pepper to taste
3 large eggs
corn oil, for frying

Grate the potatoes and onions. Put them in a colander and press out all the liquid: place a sheet of kitchen paper on top, then place a heavy saucepan on top of the paper and leave for five minutes.

Put the potato-onion mixture into a bowl and add the flour, seasoning and eggs.

Bind the mixture with the palms of your hands (take off all your jewellery first!). Take a loaded dessertspoon of the mixture, form it into a small round ball and flatten it by pressing gently. At the same time, squeeze out any excess liquid.

Put a generous amount of oil in a large frying pan and heat.

Place the *latkes* in the pan and semi-deep-fry them. When one side is lightly brown, turn over and cook the other side.

Remove from the oil with a slotted spoon, drain, then place on kitchen paper to absorb the oil.

Eat immediately, or freeze. If frozen, place on a baking tray lined with parchment and heat in a moderate oven for 15 minutes.

Make these latkes as small as you like for cocktail items, or medium-sized to serve with a main course. Delicious dipped in apple sauce.

3 salads

salads your personal trainer would be proud of

I first discovered my love for salad as a child in the 1970s. Thinking back, my mother was a nutritional genius, as she turned my brother and me on to raw vegetables with her unique 'Clock Salad'. This was a very '70s affair, straight out of *The Wonder Years*. It was a midweek supper which consisted of a large plate that had been sectioned with chopped vegetables, hard-boiled eggs and even grated cheese, like a pizza. We were allowed to choose our own 'sections'. Because my mother got us involved and excited about which vegetables we could choose, my love for salad was born.

Of course, such things can be taken to extremes, particularly when you're least expecting it – or should I say when you're expecting? When I was pregnant with my third child, for example, I immediately had a strong craving for raw cucumber (thank G-d, not doughnuts).* I sniffed cucumber, munched whole cucumbers down in one and even once had to leave a dinner party in search of a cucumber, smuggling it in and nibbling it out of my handbag!

Sometimes I still get a craving for salad and rush to my fridge to start chopping. Often, I'll use not only crispy, cold ingredients but I'll be inspired and add roasted vegetables, fruit or even warm meat to make my own personal Princess salad.

Salads are colourful, crunchy and, for the Jewish Princess, guilt-free eating on a plate – well, they're guilt-free as long as you don't add too many fattening ingredients. When ordering a salad in a restaurant, for instance, I always ask for the dressing on the side; this saves on those unwanted calories. So go on: dive in!

---

*You may be wondering why this Princess writes G-d like this. I was always taught that you should never take G-d's name in vain, even when writing. If you don't spell it out, it doesn't count...

coleslaw

serves 6

1 white cabbage, shredded
2 large carrots, grated
5 tablespoons low-fat mayonnaise

1 tablespoon double cream
salt and black pepper to taste

Mix everything together thoroughly.

If you want 'that bit extra', add one handful of flaked almonds and one handful of sultanas.

crunchy fruit and nut rice salad

serves 10

225g brown rice
225g white rice
175g dried apricots
175g dried figs
175g sultanas
salt and black pepper
110g pine nuts
110g mixed nuts
110g toasted sesame seeds

for the dressing
60ml white-wine vinegar
125ml olive oil
2 teaspoons chopped fresh
   oregano (or 1 teaspoon dried)
2 teaspoons caster sugar

First, make the dressing by combining all the dressing ingredients.

Boil the brown and white rice separately and leave to cool.

Chop all the fruits into small pieces, mix well, then add the rice and season to taste.

Stir in the dressing.

Just before serving, add the pine nuts, mixed nuts and sesame seeds and mix well.

Crunchy, colourful, and gives you loads of energy.

cucumber salad

serves 8

2 cucumbers
4 spring onions
4 tablespoons quark
(or other low-fat soft cheese)

1 bunch of chopped chives
6 mint leaves, chopped
salt and black pepper to taste

Wash and finely slice the cucumbers and spring onions.

Add the Quark, chives and mint leaves.

Mix well and season to taste.

This is a lovely, fresh-tasting salad.

green bean and tomato salad

serves 6

400g green beans
200g small, tasty tomatoes
  (sweet cherry-type)
salt and black pepper to taste

approximately 3 tablespoons
  balsamic vinegar
1 handful fresh basil leaves

Wash and trim the beans. Place in a saucepan and cover
with water.

Bring to a boil, then reduce the heat and simmer until the beans
are cooked but still have a 'bite' to them. Drain and place them
in a bowl to cool.

Wash the tomatoes. Fill a heatproof bowl with boiled water.
Place the tomatoes in the bowl and cover for five minutes.

Remove the tomatoes and peel them – the skin should come
away easily.

Chop the tomatoes and add to the beans. Season to taste with
salt and black pepper.

Add a good splash of balsamic vinegar – approximately
three tablespoons.

Add the chopped basil.

Refrigerate until ready to serve.

*This can be served as an accompaniment to a meat or fish dish,
adding colour and a crunch.*

diamond carrot salad

serves 6-8

3 packets grated carrots
(or around 1kg if you insist on
grating your own – but I don't
know why you would)
1 large orange, sliced

2 tablespoons lemon juice
2 tablespoons caster sugar
225ml fresh orange juice
110g sultanas

Mix together the first five ingredients, then add the sultanas.

This is even better if you let the sultanas soak overnight in the orange juice.

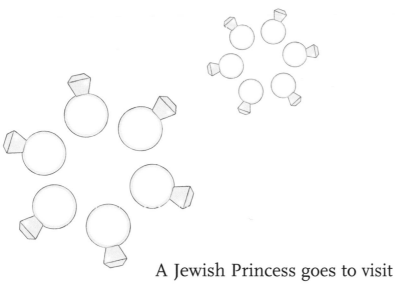

A Jewish Princess goes to visit her specialist.

She comes home and tells her husband she has been put on a very specific diet: she is only allowed carats – 2.5 and over!

oriental cabbage salad

serves 8

1 white cabbage
1 orange, cut into small pieces
1 mango, chopped
2 handfuls of raisins
125ml smooth orange juice

balsamic vinegar
olive oil
salt and black pepper
1 handful of flaked almonds

Dice the cabbage, orange and mango and mix together.

Add the raisins.

Dress with the orange juice, a good splash of balsamic vinegar and olive oil (to taste). Mix thoroughly after each addition.

Season with the salt and black pepper.

Sprinkle with the flaked almonds.

Delicious served with Sesame Chicken Balls (see page 39).

carb-loading pasta salad

serves 6-8

450g penne pasta – use brown
   pasta for a healthier dish
1 x 675g jar sweet-and-sour
   pickled cucumbers, chopped
400g tinned tuna fish

1 x 250g tin sweet corn, drained
10 tablespoons light mayonnaise
4 tablespoons tomato ketchup
salt and black pepper to taste

Cook the pasta according to the packet instructions and drain.
(Do not overcook it.)

Leave the pasta to cool.

Add the pickled cucumbers, tuna and sweet corn.

Mix the mayonnaise and ketchup together to make a Marie
Rose dressing.

Mix into the above ingredients and season to taste.

*This is very quick and easy to do. Make sure you always
keep these ingredients in your store cupboard for those
surprise lunch guests.*

chinese duck salad

serves 6

1 large duck
1 onion, peeled
1 teaspoon garlic purée
110g mixed salad leaves
1 mango, cubed
110g blanched peanuts
110g mange tout, blanched
110g bean sprouts
ready-made plum sauce
salt and black pepper to taste

for the dressing
1 teaspoon ground ginger
2 tablespoons brown sugar
1 teaspoon dijon mustard
1 tablespoon clear honey
300ml smooth orange juice

Preheat the oven to 190°C/375°F/gas mark 5.

Prick the duck all over with a fork. Put the onion and garlic purée in the duck's cavity, then place the duck on a rack over a roasting tin and cook in the preheated oven for two hours, or until the meat is cooked, turning the bird over every 30 minutes. Drain off any liquid that collects in the tin. Leave the duck to cool.

Prepare the dressing by mixing all the dressing ingredients together.

Shred the duck meat.

In a serving bowl, place the salad leaves, mango cubes, peanuts, mange tout, bean sprouts and duck meat. Pour on the dressing, toss, then season to taste.

Drizzle the plum sauce over the top just before serving.

It is so much easier to buy a ready-cooked duck!

parsley potato salad

serves 6

24 new potatoes
  (allow 4 per person)
1 bunch of flat-leaf parsley
juice of 1 lemon

virgin olive oil
125g black pitted olives, sliced
salt and black pepper to taste

Wash the potatoes and place them in a saucepan. Cover with water, bring to the boil, then turn down the temperature and simmer until the potatoes are cooked (not too soft – just so a knife will easily cut through).

Drain the potatoes and allow them to cool.

Add the chopped parsley, the lemon juice, a good drizzle of virgin olive oil, and the olives.

Season to taste.

A lovely way of making a healthier potato salad instead of a cholesterol-loaded killer!

roasted vegetable salad with goat cheese

serves 6-8

8 carrots, peeled and cut
   into batons
8 parsnips, peeled and cut
   into batons
2 sweet potatoes, peeled and
   cut into batons
2 aubergines, peeled and cut
   into batons

virgin olive oil
rock salt
1 bunch fresh coriander
1 handful of walnuts (optional)
75g soft goat cheese

Preheat the oven to 180°C/350°F/gas mark 4.

Place all the prepared vegetables in a roasting tin.

Drizzle with the olive oil.

Sprinkle with the rock salt.

Roast in the preheated oven for 45 minutes, turning the vegetables halfway through cooking.

Remove from the oven and allow to cool.

Place the vegetables into a large bowl. Add the chopped coriander and walnuts (if using).

Spoon in small balls of the goat cheese.

Drizzle with more virgin olive oil, if desired.

If you don't like goat cheese, use mozzarella balls instead.

tuscan tomato salad

serves 6

4 beef tomatoes, sliced
1 punnet small tomatoes (such as
   santa: sweet grape tomatoes),
   cut in half
6 vine tomatoes, sliced
1 red onion, finely chopped
2 bread rolls or a day-old
   baguette, cubed

1 handful of fresh basil
   leaves, chopped
4 tablespoons virgin olive oil
4 tablespoons balsamic vinegar
salt and black pepper to taste

Combine the tomatoes, onion, bread and fresh basil leaves.

Add the virgin olive oil and balsamic vinegar to taste.

Season with the salt and pepper.

*Let this marinate for at least one hour in the fridge before serving.
And do try and visit Tuscany for the real thing!*

4

soup

soup: the jewish cup of tea

In my house, we don't have teatime – we have souptime. When my children get home from school, especially in the winter, some sort of soup is always there, ready to warm and comfort them. My children know that when they open the front door, they can smell home!

Yes, soup is the perfect pep-you-up. Which makes it so very sad that so many people today never even bother to make it, thinking that it takes a zillion different ingredients and way too much time and effort. But trust me: would a true Jewish Princess include a chapter on soup in her book if that were the case? With all the fantastic vegetable and chicken stock cubes and powders* (including kosher) that are so readily available today, there's no need to spend hours making homemade stock (although you can, if you insist). Instead, you just add boiling water and get going – so perfect for Princesses!

The great thing about soup is its versatility. Whether it's served in a bowl or a mug, good soup truly is a lifesaver. Soup is the Jewish cup of tea. When you are feeling ill, cold or tired, there is nothing like a good hot bowl of homemade soup. And it doesn't just taste good – it does you good, too. In fact, chicken soup has been scientifically proven to have medicinal powers.

No wonder we've called it 'Jewish penicillin' for years!

*We JPs never use stock cubes as they don't dissolve easily. However, if this is all you have in your store cupboard, then one stock cube is roughly equal to one tablespoon of powdered stock.

bean and barley soup

serves 8

1 fowl (chicken; *see page 194*), skinned, cut into eight pieces

3 tablespoons chicken stock powder

1 x 275g tin lentils, washed and drained

2 x 450g tins butter beans, washed and drained

110g pearl barley, washed

1 large onion, peeled

4 large carrots, peeled, topped and tailed and cut into chunks

1 leek, cut into chunks

1 turnip, peeled and chopped

1 whole beef tomato (skin left on)

1 small celeriac, cubed

1 tablespoon salt

12 grinds of fresh black pepper

2.5 litres water

Place the cleaned fowl in a large saucepan and add all of the other ingredients.

Bring to the boil, then turn down the heat and let simmer with the lid on for at least three hours, or until the chicken is falling away from the bone.

Remove the tomato.

When serving, shred the chicken or remove the carcass completely (optional).

This is a meal in a bowl – and it's also low on the glycaemic index.

bloody mary borscht

serves 8

12 medium, raw beetroot,
  peeled and cubed
1 medium onion
1 medium carrot
1.2 litres hot water mixed with 2
  tablespoons of vegetable stock

3 tablespoons caster sugar
black pepper to taste
1 litre tomato juice
worcestershire sauce to taste
splash of vodka

Peel the beetroot and onion, and peel, top and tail the carrot.
Place the vegetables in a large saucepan.

Add the water and stock mixture, then the sugar, and season with
plenty of black pepper.

Bring to the boil, then turn down the heat and simmer until the
vegetables are soft. Remove the carrot and onion.

When cooled, add the tomato juice, blend well, then run
the liquid through a sieve.

Add the Worcestershire sauce to taste, then the splash of vodka.
Refrigerate until ready to serve.

Serve chilled.

*When serving this soup, add a little jug of vodka for people to
help themselves. This is a fabulous, fun soup (but watch out if
you're wearing white...).*

broccoli soup

serves 6

75g unsalted butter
2 medium onions, diced
675g broccoli, trimmed
  and cut into florets
50g plain flour

1.2 litres vegetable stock (make
  this with 2 heaped tablespoons
  of vegetable bouillon powder)
1 pinch of nutmeg
salt and pepper to taste
300ml milk

In a large saucepan over a gentle heat, melt the butter, making sure it doesn't burn.

Sauté the chopped onions until soft. Add the broccoli and cook for five minutes, or until just tender.

Stir in the flour and cook gently for one minute. Remove from the heat and gradually stir in the stock.

Bring to the boil and then reduce the heat. Cover and simmer for 15 to 20 minutes, or until the vegetables are tender.

Add the nutmeg. Season to taste with the salt and black pepper.

Put the soup into a food processor or blender and whizz until smooth.

Reheat gently and slowly stir in the milk.

A delicious and creamy soup full of vitamins – and the children won't even realize it!

A Jewish Princess goes into a restaurant
and sees they have fish soup on the menu.
She calls the waiter over and asks:
'Does the fish soup contain shellfish?'
'Yes,' says the waiter.
She calls over another waiter and asks:
'Does the fish soup contain shellfish?'
'Yes,' says the waiter.
She calls over a third waiter and asks again:
'Does the fish soup contain shellfish?'
'No,' says the waiter.

The Jewish Princess replies: 'I'll have it!'

no shellfish fish soup

serves 8

1 onion, chopped
4 carrots, peeled, topped
  and tailed, then chopped
3 leeks, chopped
2 potatoes, peeled and cubed
2 fish stock cubes
1 teaspoon curry powder
1 teaspoon cinnamon
1 pinch of saffron, softened in
  a little boiling water

half a bottle of dry white wine
2 tablespoons brandy
1 carrot, peeled, topped,
  tailed and grated
1 leek, cut into thin batons
150ml double cream
600g mixed skinless fish fillets
  (salmon, cod and haddock),
  cut into chunks
salt and black pepper to taste

Place the onion, chopped carrots, chopped leeks and the cubed potatoes into a large saucepan.

Dissolve the fish stock cubes in 600ml of boiling water and pour over the vegetables. Add more water if the vegetables are not covered.

Add the curry powder, cinnamon and saffron.

Bring to the boil, then turn down the heat and simmer until the vegetables are soft (approximately 20 minutes).

Process the soup with a hand blender.

In a separate saucepan, pour in the wine and brandy and simmer until the liquid starts to reduce.

Add the grated carrot and the batons of leek. Cook gently until the vegetables are soft.

Add this mixture to the main soup.

Stir in the double cream and add the fish. Cook on a low heat for a further ten minutes, or until the fish is cooked and flaky.

Season to taste with salt and black pepper.

This is delicious served with French bread that has been sliced and toasted with grated Emmental cheese on top and tomato aioli, which is a garlic mayonnaise with a tomato twist.

To make the aioli, just take 4 tablespoons of mayonnaise, add a half-teaspoon of tomato paste, a half-teaspoon of garlic paste and a half-teaspoon of Dijon mustard, and voilà: it will take you straight to the South of France.

honey-roasted butternut squash soup

serves 8

2kg butternut squash, cut into
  7.5cm wedges and deseeded
3 tablespoons olive oil
garlic purée
salt and pepper to taste
4 onions, finely chopped
4 carrots, topped, tailed and
  finely chopped

2 teaspoons dried parsley
4 tablespoons vegetable bouillon
  powder dissolved in 2.4 litres
  of boiled water
1½ tablespoons runny honey

Preheat the oven to 240°C/475°F/gas mark 9.

Brush the squash wedges with a little olive oil and place them
on a roasting tray. Dot the wedges with garlic purée (about one
teaspoon per wedge), then season with salt and pepper and roast
for 45 minutes in the oven. Cool, then scoop the flesh off the skin.

Heat the three tablespoons of olive oil in a large saucepan. Add
the onions and carrots and cook gently for ten to 15 minutes, or
until the vegetables are soft but not brown. Add the parsley.

Pour the stock onto the vegetables, bring to the boil, then turn
down the heat and simmer for 20 minutes, or until tender.

Add the squash to the stock and veg. Simmer for five more minutes.

Blend until smooth, stir in the honey, and gently heat through.
Check the seasoning and adjust if necessary.

*When you cut the butternut squash, be careful, as they're very
tough-skinned. You don't want to end up in casualty!*

jerusalem artichoke soup

serves 8

4 tablespoons olive oil
600g red onions, chopped
600g potatoes, peeled
  and chopped
1kg jerusalem artichokes,
  peeled and chopped

2 tablespoons vegetable
  bouillon powder
1.2 litres water
salt and black pepper to taste
300ml soya milk

Heat the olive oil in a large saucepan. Add the red onions and cook, stirring constantly, until soft.

Add the potatoes and artichokes, cover, and sweat for ten minutes (this means the vegetables – not you going out for a run!).

Add the stock powder, water and seasoning. Simmer on a low heat until the vegetables are soft (approximately 30 minutes).

Liquidize the soup and stir in the soya milk.

Check the seasoning and adjust if necessary.

Don't be scared of Jerusalem artichokes. Underneath the knobbly skin of these unusual, ugly vegetables lies a true delicacy.

leek and potato soup

serves 8

1½ tablespoons olive oil
2 onions, finely chopped
7 large leeks, washed, peeled
   and finely chopped
4 large potatoes, cut into
   1cm chunks
2 level tablespoons vegetable
   bouillon powder

2.4 litres water
sea salt and black pepper to taste
1 teaspoon ground nutmeg
300ml double cream
2 tablespoons fresh
   chives, chopped

In a large saucepan, heat the olive oil. Add the onions and leeks and gently sauté until soft.

Add the potatoes, the vegetable bouillon powder, water, salt and pepper. Bring to the boil, turn down the heat and simmer, covered, for 20 to 25 minutes, or until the vegetables are soft.

Stir in the nutmeg.

Remove from the heat and allow to cool.

Liquidize thoroughly and stir in the cream.

Check the seasoning and adjust if necessary.

To serve, stir in a little swirl of cream in each bowl and garnish with chopped chives.

This can be made the day before to allow the flavours to infuse – and to give Jewish Princesses a little extra shopping time.

mushy pea soup

serves 8

1.8kg frozen petits pois or
    other green peas
1 large onion, chopped
3 leeks, sliced
1 tablespoon dried parsley

chicken or vegetable stock
    powder – approximately
    3 tablespoons
salt and black pepper to taste
mint leaves, for decoration

In a large saucepan, place the petits pois, onion and leeks.
Add the parsley and stock powder, fill the saucepan with enough
water to cover the vegetables, then bring to the boil. Turn down
the heat and let simmer, covered, until the peas are very soft.

Using a hand blender, liquidize the soup. Add the salt and
pepper to taste.

When the soup has cooled, push it through a sieve – this is
annoying, but it makes the soup taste incredible! To serve, put
a few mint leaves in each bowl for decoration.

*To make a fun dinner, ask your husband to go get some fish and
chips – so now you have your fish, chips and peas!*

onion soup

serves 6

5 teaspoons olive oil
4 medium onions, sliced
4 teaspoons caster sugar
1.7 litres water

3 tablespoons vegetable
  bouillon powder
2 teaspoons marmite
2 tablespoons sherry
salt and black pepper to taste

In a large saucepan, heat the olive oil, then add the onions and sweat them until soft.

Add the rest of the ingredients.

Bring to the boil, then lower the heat and cover. Leave the soup to simmer on a very low heat for about 30 minutes.

Season to taste.

When serving, toast thick slices of French bread and melt grated Cheddar or Emmental cheese on them. Chop them up and place them as croûtons in the middle of the soup.

parsnip and apple soup

serves 6

1 onion, diced
450g parsnips, washed
   and cubed
1.5 litres boiled water

3 tablespoons vegetable
   bouillon powder
5 eating apples, peeled and sliced
250ml double cream

Put the onions, parsnips, water and bouillon powder in a large saucepan. Bring to the boil, lower the heat, cover and simmer for 20 minutes, or until the parsnips are soft.

Meanwhile, put the peeled apples in a separate microwave-able bowl, cover with two tablespoons of water and cook on high for two minutes. When you take the apples out of the microwave, check that they are soft.

Add the apples to the vegetables.

Liquidize the soup and stir in the cream to serve.

This one will keep your dinner guests guessing, trying to work out all the ingredients.

tomato soup with basil-infused croûtons

serves 6

2 tablespoons olive oil
4 shallots, peeled and chopped
3 celery sticks, washed
  and chopped
2 carrots, peeled, topped,
  tailed and chopped
1 large handful of torn
  basil leaves
1 large bunch of sage leaves
2 bay leaves
3 x 400g tins chopped
  tomatoes in their juice

1.2 litres water mixed with
  2 tablespoons of vegetable
  bouillon powder
3.5 tablespoons caster sugar
salt and black pepper to taste
splash of olive oil

for the croûtons
day-old French bread
1 garlic clove
6 tablespoons olive oil
1 handful of torn basil leaves

First, make the croûtons.

Preheat the oven to 140°C/275°F/gas mark 1.

Slice the French bread into thin slices. Rub both sides with garlic.

In a bowl using a hand blender, blend together the olive oil
and basil.

Brush onto one side of the bread slices.

Place in the preheated oven for 20 minutes, turning halfway
through, until the bread has dried out.

Place in an airtight container.

To make the soup, heat the olive oil in a large saucepan. Add the shallots and sauté.

As they become translucent, add the celery, carrots, basil, sage and bay leaves.

When the vegetables are soft, add all the other ingredients.

Reduce the heat, cover and simmer on a low heat for a good hour or so.

Liquidize the soup.

To make it extra-special, pour it through a sieve before serving.

Serve with basil-infused croûtons.

Tomato soup is hard to get right, but this is JP perfect! Serve with croûtons and a basil leaf to decorate.

diaspora dishes: london to new york

And now, an aside. While you recover from all those luscious soups, salads and appetizers, it's time for a little break before diving into the main courses. So put your feet up for a minute and relax while reading the following. It's educational (well, a *bissel*...).

Maybe it's because of the Jewish people's history of dispersal, traditionally known as the Diaspora, but whatever the reason, the modern Jewish Princess still loves to roam – or should I say Rome, Paris, Milan, London and New York? Cities like these, after all, are centres of cultural importance, home to resplendent art galleries, shops, magnificent museums, shops, incredible restaurants – and did I mention the most amazing shops?

To a JP, this intoxicating combination is always a recipe for success. Whenever I return from any holiday, I'm always motivated to try out in my own kitchen all the foods I have eaten and loved abroad. Almost as soon as the tyres hit the runway, I find myself running to my nearest supermarket to stock up on new foods I have experienced (OK, so I'm in the shops again), simply to bring back the flavour of wherever it is I've just been.

Throughout history, Jewish Princesses have loved to travel, and our food contains tastes and flavours that come from all over the world. This makes Jewish cooking terrifically exciting, as this hotpot of global flavours produces the most extraordinary dishes. From Spain to South Africa, London to Lithuania, Ashkenazi and Sephardi Jews (*see* Yiddish/English Glossary, page 210) have concocted a unique style of cooking that takes a little of this and a little of that to create food which family and friends adore.

So next time you come home from holiday, if you can't fit the sun into your luggage due to the other purchases you made, just remember all those flavours you tasted and savoured. With a bit of culinary creativity, you can be transported back to that special place again and again.

5 meat

meat: not always a 'rare' kosher treat

No matter how far she may wander or roam, ultimately a Jewish Princess will have to make some key decisions.

The first is: 'Do I keep a kosher home?'
The second: 'Do I keep kosher when I go out to eat?'
The third: 'Do I eat only in kosher restaurants, or eat only certain fish or vegetarian dishes and go to non-kosher restaurants?'

Everyone finds her own level. Often it relates to how you were brought up or how guilty (ever heard of Jewish guilt?) you might feel if your fork touched a forbidden food. For a Jewish Princess, it is up to her to find which foods may turn her into a frog.

I made my decision and decided to keep a kosher home. Therefore the relationship I have with my butcher is of paramount importance. Not, obviously, as important as the relationship I have with my hairdresser, but close.

I have spent many years searching for an excellent butcher. This search was a bit like my dating years. I have 'courted' a few butchers in my time, but I had to chuck them for various reasons: sending me a hairy chicken; not saving me eggs for the chicken soup (a great kosher delicacy – these golden eggs are in short supply and I am not prepared to do my butcher any favours to get them). A tough piece of beef was definitely a chucking-out offence, but the worst crime of all was when a butcher completely ripped me off for a crown of lamb by charging me an exorbitant price.

I am afraid there was A Scene.

Finally, however, after much cruising and shmoozing, I found the perfect butcher. Of course, we are on first-name terms; I know all about his family, (well, most of them work in the shop). My chickens are hairless, my beef is always tender and delicious, and he always saves me the precious golden eggs for my chicken soup – *without* any favours!

Why am I telling you all this? Simple: my friends and family are Carnivores, with a capital 'C'. We just *love* meat.

Also, many of my friends have made the decision to keep kosher when dining out, and they will eat only fish and vegetarian dishes in non-kosher restaurants. They spend their evenings eyeing up pieces of beef and chicken that come flying out of the kitchen and past them, carried by deaf waiters (Don't you find that this is a common affliction affecting most waiters? It seems to be a requirement for the job...). So when my kosher-keeping friends come to my home for dinner, it is a really special treat to tuck into meat – and there is nothing more satisfying than to take out of the oven a juicy joint and know that my guests will truly appreciate it.

Now I know that, like fine wine, there is a certain amount of snobbery regarding the cooking of meat, but I have to say, give the people what they want. If they don't like it rare now, they never will. And if they love it well done, then you should serve it that way.

It is the *enjoyment* of the meat that is everything.

So when I have guests, there are no deaf waiters (I do occasionally have a waitress, but that is only for very large gatherings), the meat is always cooked to my friends' requirements, and when I see an empty plate I know that I, for one, will get a big 'well done'.

A Jewish Princess went on a
walking holiday. She power-walked
from Egypt to Israel.

It took her forty years, but boy,
did she have great legs by the end!

chicken curry in a hurry

serves 2

3 tablespoons olive oil
2 onions, diced
2 chicken breast fillets, diced
1 x 175g tin tomatoes in
   tomato juice
3 teaspoons medium
   curry powder

50g sultanas
1 banana, sliced
1 x 175ml tin creamed coconut
1 teaspoon caster sugar
salt and pepper to taste
mango chutney to serve

Heat a wok or large, heavy frying pan.

Add the olive oil.

Add the chopped onions and sauté until brown, then add the diced chicken fillets and stir until cooked.

Add the tomatoes and curry powder to taste, then stir in the sultanas and the sliced banana and cook for approximately three minutes.

Add the creamed coconut and the caster sugar and continue cooking until the liquid has reduced and a creamy sauce is left (approximately ten minutes).

Season to taste with salt and pepper.

Serve with cooked rice and mango chutney on the side for a hot, romantic dinner for two.

chicken schnitzel in wine and spritely lemonade

serves 10

10 chicken fillets
3 large eggs, beaten
breadcrumbs or matzo meal
olive oil, for frying

for the marinade
12 tablespoons white wine
8 tablespoons sprite
4 garlic cloves, crushed
2 tablespoons lemon juice
1 x 15g packet of fresh chives

Mix all the marinade ingredients together and pour over the chicken fillets. Leave to marinate for a couple of hours – or even better, overnight.

Dip the chicken fillets into the beaten egg, then in the breadcrumbs or matzo meal.

Fry in the olive oil until golden brown and serve.

This unusual concoction always goes down well, even with difficult eaters. Try it and see!

gedempte chicken

serves 6

3 tablespoons corn oil
1 red onion, diced
1 white onion, diced
1 chicken, cut into 8 pieces
enough plain flour to coat the
   chicken (approximately 150g)
500ml water

1 x 500g tin passata
2 garlic cloves, pressed
2 bouquets garni
salt and black pepper to taste
6 large potatoes, cut into quarters
   and parboiled

Heat the oil and fry the onions in a large wok until they are as dark as possible without burning them.

Dip the chicken pieces in the plain flour and fry them with the onions until the chicken is slightly brown.

Transfer the chicken and onions into a deep saucepan and add the water, passata, garlic, the bouquets garni, salt and pepper.

Bring to the boil, then turn down the heat, cover and let it simmer very gently until the chicken is soft and dark-brown in colour. This will take at least one and a half hours.

Halfway through the cooking, add the partly boiled potatoes, which will continue to cook in the meat juices and will turn a dark brown.

Whenever I make this, I feel like my grandmother-over-sholom is with us at the table, enjoying the fact that all the family are together.

A Jewish Princess goes into her butcher's to pick up her chickens. 'Are they in yet?' She enquires.

'No,' says the butcher. 'They'll be back from the dry cleaners in two minutes!'

moroccan chicken

serves 6

vegetable oil, enough to fry
 (approximately 4 tablespoons)
1 tablespoon tomato purée
2 teaspoons garlic purée
2 teaspoons cumin
1 teaspoon cinnamon
1 chicken cut, into 8 pieces
4 medium onions, peeled and
 sliced (use frozen if you like)

18 dried apricots
3 preserved lemons
 (found in most supermarkets)
300ml water
1 tablespoon chicken stock
 powder or 1 chicken stock cube
salt and black pepper to taste

Preheat the oven to 180°C/350°F/gas mark 4.

Heat the vegetable oil, then add the tomato purée, garlic purée, cumin and cinnamon.

Quickly fry each piece of chicken.

Place the chicken pieces in a roasting dish.

Fry the onions in the remaining oil until they are soft. Do not burn!

Pour the onions over the chicken.

Add the dried apricots, preserved lemons, and water mixed with the chicken stock powder (or cube) to the bottom of a roasting tin. Season with the salt and pepper.

Roast in the preheated oven for at least one hour, or until the juices run clear.

Lovely served with couscous. Just don't do those belly-dancing exercises straight afterwards…

poussin with apple and sage

serves 6

3 poussin (allow at least half a
  poussin per person)
3 gala (or similar) apples, halved
6 fresh sage leaves per poussin
shallots, peeled
carrots, topped, tailed, peeled
  and cut into chunks

chicken stock, approximately 500ml
salt and black pepper to taste
honey
olive oil
fresh oregano leaves

Preheat the oven to 180°C/350°F/gas mark 4.

Clean each poussin.

Stuff each one with two apple halves and six sage leaves.

In the bottom of a roasting tin, place the peeled whole shallots
and peeled chunks of carrots (as many as you want).

Place the poussins in the roasting dish and pour in enough
chicken stock so that the dish is at least half-full.

Season the poussin with salt and black pepper. Rub a little honey
and olive oil into the skin of each poussin.

Sprinkle fresh oregano leaves over the top.

Roast in the preheated oven for 45 to 60 minutes, or until the skin
is golden.

*This is easy to serve, and the result looks like a celebrity chef has
invaded your kitchen.*

cumberland cutlets

serves 4 to 6 *(depending on how many men you're serving!)*

8 lamb cutlets
salt and pepper to season
2 medium eggs, beaten
fine matzo meal or
  fine breadcrumbs

for the sauce
450ml chicken stock
9 rounded tablespoons redcurrant
  (or cranberry) jelly
juice of 4 oranges
1 orange, sliced, for garnish
5 teaspoons lemon juice

Preheat the oven to 200°C/400°F/gas mark 6.

Trim off most of the fat from the lamb cutlets, then sprinkle with salt and pepper.

Dip the cutlets into the beaten egg, then into the breadcrumbs or matzo meal. Put in a baking tin side by side.

To make the sauce, heat all the ingredients together until smooth and pour half over the cutlets. Cover with foil.

Cook in the preheated oven for one hour, then add the remaining sauce. Turn the oven down to 180°C/350°F/gas mark 4 and cook for a further 20 minutes.

Garnish with the orange segments.

Not, sadly, named after the Cumberland Hotel in Bournemouth, a kosher hotel that existed in the 1970s which was renowned for its copious amounts of food.

sticky lamb chops

serves 6

6 tablespoons clear honey
6 tablespoons tomato ketchup
6 tablespoons dark soy sauce

6 tablespoons water
12 medium lamb chops

Combine the honey, ketchup, soy sauce and water in a bowl.

Arrange the lamb chops lying side by side in an ovenproof dish.

Pour the sauce over the meat and place in the fridge to marinate for half an hour (or longer if desired).

When ready to cook, bake uncovered in an oven preheated to 160°C/325°F/gas mark 3 for at least an hour.

Check that the cutlets are not drying out, and turn throughout cooking, basting with the marinade.

Junior JPs' favourite.

shepherd's pie

serves 6

1 onion, diced
10g non-dairy margarine
200g mushrooms,
    peeled and sliced
450g minced lamb
1 x 400g tin chopped tomatoes
6 bay leaves
salt and black pepper to taste

for the topping
1kg sweet potatoes,
    peeled and diced
30g non-dairy margarine
1 tablespoon tomato purée
½ teaspoon cumin
½ teaspoon nutmeg
salt and black pepper to taste

Preheat the oven to 190°C/375°F/gas mark 5.

Fry the onion in the margarine until slightly brown.

Add the mushrooms and continue to fry until soft.

Add the meat, the tinned tomatoes and the bay leaves and simmer on a low heat for one hour. Don't forget to season with salt and black pepper at this point!

Transfer the lamb to an ovenproof dish.

Next, make the topping. Put the sweet potatoes in a saucepan with just enough water to cover, then boil them until soft.

Drain off the water and leave the potatoes to cool.

Add the rest of the topping ingredients to the potatoes and mash thoroughly. Spread the topping over the cooked lamb.

Bake the lamb in the preheated oven for approximately 25 minutes, or until the topping has become crispy.

When you make this dish you won't need a shepherd to get everyone to the table!

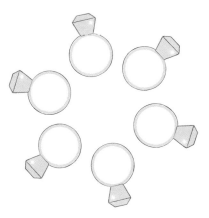

brisket with prunes

serves 6

1.5kg brisket (unpickled)
2 parsnips
6 carrots
2 onions

black pepper to taste
1 bay leaf
12 dried pitted prunes
50g onion soup mix

Preheat the oven to 150°C/300°F/gas mark 2.

Wash the brisket and place the meat in a roasting tin filled halfway with water.

Peel all the vegetables and leave them whole. Season well with black pepper and add them to the roasting tin.

Add the rest of the ingredients.

Cover with foil and cook in the preheated oven for three hours, turning the brisket every hour, until the meat is soft.

A great dish for impressing your guests, especially when served with couscous. As a bonus, you can leave it in the oven and have a little 'me time' (three hours' worth!) before they arrive.

you say corned beef, i say salt beef

serves 8

2kg centre pickled brisket
1 onion, washed but not peeled
6 peppercorns

1 bay leaf, split either end
 to infuse
1 teaspoon caster sugar

Place the washed salt beef in a large saucepan and cover with water. Cover with the pan lid and bring to the boil.

When scum appears, throw away the first water and refill with fresh, clean cold water – enough to cover the beef.

Add the onion, peppercorns, bay leaf and sugar and bring to the boil.

When scum reappears, skim this away with a large spoon. Place the lid half on the saucepan and continue to simmer for approximately two and a half hours, or until the beef is tender.

Add boiling water to the saucepan if the liquid falls below the line of the beef.

To see if the beef has cooked, test it by piercing with a fork. If it comes out easily, it's ready.

Either serve straight away or allow the beef to get cold.

When cold, slice thinly and reheat in the microwave with a little of the liquor on top.

For a great sandwich, deli-style, serve salt beef on rye bread with English mustard and pickles. Salt beef and latkes (see page 41) are the Jewish 'eggs and bacon'.

cholent
(meat stew with pulses and potatoes)

serves 8

2kg stewing beef (I use top rib)
6 onions, sliced
175g pearl barley
6 large potatoes, cut into quarters
2 bay leaves
235g (drained weight) tinned
  cannellini beans
235g (drained weight) tinned
  butter beans

235g (drained weight) tinned
  borlotti beans
350g passata (or a large can of
  chopped tomatoes)
plenty of black pepper
2 teaspoon salt
2 teaspoons dark brown sugar
3 carrots, peeled, topped
  and tailed
2 tablespoons beef stock powder
  or 2 beef stock cubes

Preheat the oven to 200°C/400°F/gas mark 6.

Place all the ingredients in a large, heavy, ovenproof pot or dish (I use a large saucepan) with the beef in the centre and the potatoes around the beef.

Pour in enough water to cover all the ingredients, then cover and cook in the preheated oven for one hour.

Turn the heat down to 150°C/300°F/gas mark 2 and leave in the oven for the next seven hours.

If you're going to leave the dish to cook longer, just turn the heat down even more.

I know this breaks the ten-ingredient rule, but it's allowed due to the fact that it is simply a matter of opening cans (just watch your fingernails, of course!).

This wonderful stew is traditionally made on Friday before the Sabbath, and left in the oven overnight, ready for lunch the next day. Absolutely delicious.

tzimmes
(braised beef and carrots)

serves *as many as you like!*

1kg carrots, peeled and cubed
   (or buy prepared)
3 tablespoons soft
   light brown sugar
beef brisket or rolled rib (any size,
   depending on how many you
   want to feed)

salt and pepper to taste
olive oil, for searing
4 tablespoons cornflour
1kg potatoes, peeled and
   sliced thickly
1 x 450g tin golden syrup

Preheat the oven to 140°C/275°F/gas mark 1.

Boil the carrots until *al dente* in water to which one tablespoon of brown sugar has been added.

Season the meat with salt and pepper.

Coat a large frying pan with a little oil, heat it, and sear the meat.

In a bowl, put two tablespoons of brown sugar and two tablespoons of cornflour. Stir them together.

Drain the carrots, reserving the liquid.

Line a large, deep, heatproof casserole with a layer of carrots. Sprinkle them with the sugar and cornflour mixture.

Place the seared meat on top of the carrots in the middle of the casserole.

Sprinkle two tablespoons of cornflour over the meat.

Continue layering with carrots and potatoes, seasoning each layer as you go.

Pour the reserved carrot liquor into the casserole, making sure the meat is covered. Add water if needed.

Pour in the golden syrup, then cover the dish tightly with aluminium foil to keep it from drying out.

Cook in the preheated oven for at least eight hours. Keep checking to see if it needs some more water.

This dish is best made the day before so that you can leave it to cook overnight on a low heat. It's great to serve in front of the fire on a cold, dark evening with a big glass of red wine.

ye olde steak pie

serves 6

1kg diced steak
1 punnet button mushrooms
25g onion soup mix
150ml kiddush wine
  (or you can use
  your own red plonk)
150ml water
1 garlic clove
6 shallots, peeled
  and left whole
4 small (or 2 large) carrots,
  topped, tailed and chopped

1 x large 400g tin
  chopped tomatoes
1 teaspoon caster sugar

for the pastry
500g puff pastry
1 medium egg, lightly whisked
black pepper to taste

Preheat the oven to 120°C/250°F/gas mark ½.

Place all the ingredients in a round casserole dish.

Cover with a lid or foil, and cook slowly in the oven for at least three hours, or until the meat is soft.

Leave to cool. Check the seasoning and adjust if necessary.

Roll out the pastry (unless you buy pastry already rolled – 'Great move!' I say).

Paint beaten egg around the rim of the casserole. Add the pastry and press down the sides to seal.

Brush beaten egg over the top and make a cross in the centre with your knife (this stops the pastry going soggy).

Preheat the oven to 220°C/425°F/gas mark 7 and bake for five minutes, then reduce the heat to 190°C/375°F/gas mark 5 and bake for a further 30 minutes, until the gravy is bubbling up.

If you're concerned about the pastry (especially if you're watching your carbs), just make the casserole on its own.

6

fish

f.i.s.h. = finally i saved him

After Hubby and I had been going out for a few weeks, I was sure he would be ready to propose once he had been to our house for a Friday night dinner.

This, of course, led to the inevitable problem of having to consider that maybe it wasn't *me* he fell in love with, but the meal my mother served him...

But anyway.

The reason I felt I was on to a sure thing was simple. Because his mother, for some very bizarre reason, served fish on Friday nights (maybe she thought they were Catholic?), Hubby had been deprived of the joys of chicken soup, chopped liver and roast chicken all his life (*see* 'The Ultimate Friday Night Dinner', page 187). So when he arrived at my house and saw the table, when he was served piping-hot chicken soup and all the rest, he saw in my mother the promise of the woman I would become.

That night, instead of eating it, Hubby-To-Be *turned into* fish – he had been well and truly caught!

Due to the fish that was forced upon him, my lovely husband suffered for many years with a fish phobia. After all, if *you* had been given fish that looked like it had just escaped from a hospital ward (his mother wasn't the most imaginative cook), you, too, would find yourself fearing fish.

So Hubby hated fish with a passion, and whenever he had to eat at his mother's after we were married, she just served him a hard-boiled egg, as, by this time, she had finally given up. (Being a true Jewish Princess, I always politely ate my hospital fare.)

Because of his fish fear, I decided that fish should not be forced back into my husband's life. However, I didn't want to deprive myself or my children of that excellent brain food. After all, they would have school entrance exams to sit, so they would need every little bit of help they could get (including the odd hour or so of private tuition – competition is very high).

So with a few clever recipes, I was sure that my beloved could grow to have a fondness for fish. Slowly, over the years, and with the aim of preserving my husband's heart muscle, I have managed – with patience, coaxing and little phrases such as, 'Go on: just one little bite' (well, you know all men are little boys at heart) – to persuade him to eat fish.

And yes, you better believe it: now he actually *likes* it!

It really took some Princess perseverance, but after all, he *was* my soulmate. I knew that, with the right treatment, he could find a plaice – sorry, make that *place* – in his heart for fish.

So if you have a member of your family who says 'I hate x,y and z', don't give up. After all, sushi at first sight takes some getting used to; now people are in love with it the world over.

I mean, whoever thought *my* Prince would actually *challish* for a piece of raw salmon?

What's a Jewish Princess's
favourite wine?

I want to go to Marbella!

fish tempura

serves 4

2 skinless salmon fillets
2 skinless cod fillets
salt and black pepper to taste
150g tempura batter mix
  (this can be purchased at
  most large supermarkets or
  a japanese food store)

vegetable oil
16 baby corn pieces or
  baby carrots
soy sauce

Cut each piece of salmon and cod into four strips.

Season the fish with salt and black pepper.

Mix up the tempura batter.

Coat the fish with tempura batter and fry (making sure there is enough oil to cover the fish) until golden brown.

Coat the vegetables in the batter and fry until golden brown.

Place all the fish and vegetables on kitchen paper to soak up any excess oil.

Serve with soy sauce on the side to dip.

If you have chopsticks in the house, use these instead of knives and forks – it's much more fun!

haddock kedgeree

serves 4

2 large skinless fillets natural
  smoked haddock
1 tablespoon vegetable
  bouillon powder
350g rice
110g unsalted butter

1 teaspoon curry powder
1 handful of chopped parsley
3 medium hard-boiled
  eggs, chopped
425ml double cream
salt and black pepper to taste

Place the haddock into a large saucepan and cover with water.

Add the vegetable bouillon powder, and cook over a low heat until the haddock is poached.

Remove the fish and leave to cool. Retain the fish stock, but set aside one ladle of it for later.

Add the rice to the fish stock and cook, adding more water if necessary. Set aside when cooked.

Turn on a medium heat and drop half of the butter into another saucepan. Add the curry powder, chunked haddock, and parsley and sauté gently, stirring constantly.

Add half the cooked rice and keep stirring. Add the remainder of the rice and the rest of the butter. Keep stirring.

Add the chopped egg, the ladle of fish stock and the cream.

Season to taste with black pepper and serve immediately.

Haddock kedgeree is a bit like marmite – you love it or you hate it. So be careful who you serve it to!

hot and spicy fish

serves 6

for the fish balls
2 large eggs
1 large potato (approximately
    225g), peeled and boiled
    until soft
1 tablespoon dried parsley
1 teaspoon paprika
1 teaspoon ground nutmeg
1 red onion, diced
1 teaspoon garlic purée
500g white fish, minced
salt and pepper to taste

for the sauce
2 x 400g tins chopped tomatoes
55g chopped fresh basil
1 tablespoon tomato purée
2 teaspoons curry powder
2 teaspoons caster sugar
salt and pepper to taste
3 tablespoons single cream

corn oil, for frying

Place all the fish-ball ingredients in a food processor and process until everything is well-mixed.

Let the mixture rest for 15 minutes.

To make the fish balls, wet your hands with water, then take a heaped teaspoon of the mixture and shape it into an oval ball.

In a frying pan, fry the fish balls in just enough corn oil to cover until they are a golden colour.

Drain on kitchen paper to absorb any excess oil, then place in an ovenproof dish.

To make the sauce, put all the sauce ingredients into a food processor and mix thoroughly.

Preheat the oven to 180°C/350°F/gas mark 4.

Pour the sauce over the fish balls and bake in the preheated oven for 40 minutes.

These are great without the sauce to serve with drinks. Or instead of serving them as a main course, serve a smaller amount as a forspeise (see Yiddish/English Glossary, page 211).

individual salmon en croute

serves 4

150ml double cream
1 x 250g tin asparagus
1 bunch watercress, chopped
1 bunch of dill, chopped
1 pinch of nutmeg

salt and black pepper to taste
500g ready-made puff pastry
4 skinless salmon fillets
1 medium egg, beaten

Preheat the oven to 220°C/425°F/gas mark 7.

In a large bowl, add the cream, asparagus, chopped watercress, chopped dill, nutmeg, salt and pepper (season well). Mix with a hand blender.

Roll out the pastry to about half a centimetre thickness.

Season the salmon with a little salt, then place it on the pastry. Cut a square large enough to cover the salmon and make a parcel.

Spoon the asparagus mixture on top of the salmon and close the pastry to make the parcel. Press down the edges.

Brush on the beaten egg and score the top of the pastry.

Place on greaseproof paper.

Bake in the preheated oven for ten to 15 minutes.

If you do not wish to use individual fillets, just use a larger piece of salmon, or make smaller ones to serve as canapés. Once the salmon en croute is cooked, slice it into pieces to serve.

lemon fish cakes

serves 6

2 medium eggs
4 slices of white bread,
   without crusts
1 tablespoon dried parsley
1 teaspoon hot paprika
1 teaspoon ground nutmeg
1 garlic clove, chopped

1 tablespoon wholegrain mustard
1 tablespoon lemon juice
500g white fish, minced
salt and black pepper

corn oil, for frying
mango chutney, for serving

Put all the ingredients, except the oil and chutney, into a food processor and process until they are all well-mixed.

Let the mixture rest for 15 minutes.

Using a heaped teaspoon, drop a spoonful of the mixture at a time into enough oil to cover the cakes and fry until they are golden in colour.

Serve on a bed of basmati rice with mango chutney.

paella marbella

serves 6

2 tablespoons vegetable oil,
  for frying
1 green chilli, deseeded
  and diced
1 medium red pepper, deseeded
  and chopped
2 teaspoons garlic purée
2 large beef tomatoes, sliced
  and cubed
1.25 litres vegetable or fish stock
2 generous pinches of saffron

200g fresh salmon
300g fresh cod
350g rice
150g fresh tuna
115g black olives, pitted
  and drained
salt and black pepper to taste
225g frozen peas
1 red onion, peeled and sliced
  into rings

Coat a large, deep frying pan with the vegetable oil (I usually use a wok), then add the chilli, pepper and garlic and cook for five minutes over a moderate heat, stirring the ingredients continuously.

Next, add the tomatoes and continue stirring for another five minutes.

Pour in the stock along with the saffron and simmer for ten minutes, keeping an eye on the mixture by stirring occasionally.

Add all the fish except for the tuna and simmer for another ten minutes.

Add the rice to the pan, mix it in with the contents and simmer for another ten minutes.

Add the tuna, salt and pepper and olives and cook for a further five minutes.

Add the peas and cook for a further five minutes.

In a separate frying pan, sauté the onion rings in a little olive oil and add on top of the paella to garnish.

So I know this recipe breaks the ten-ingredient rule, but even JPs know that rules are meant to be broken. This dish is so easy to make and looks FABULOUS! Mucho delicious!

sole colbert

serves 2

4 lemon sole fillets
salt and black pepper
flour, for dusting
2 bananas, sliced horizontally

110g unsalted butter
1 tablespoon vegetable oil
mango chutney, to serve

Wash and dry the sole fillets.

Season with salt and black pepper.

Put the flour on a plate and lightly dip the sole fillets into the flour, then pat off any surplus.

Dip the bananas into the flour, also patting off any surplus.

Heat a frying pan and melt the butter with the oil.

Fry the sole fillets gently, making sure that both sides are brown.

Do the same with the bananas.

Arrange on a plate, with the mango chutney on the side.

Husbands, boyfriends and lovers will adore this dish. Just don't invite them all over at the same time...

A Jewish Princess
went fishing.

She came home with
a new place!

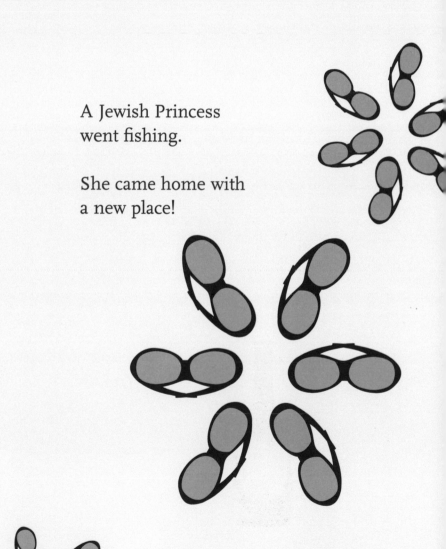

sophisticated fish pie

serves 8

2 onions, diced
2-3 tablespoons vegetable oil
2 aubergines, cubed
4 carrots, topped, tailed
  and cubed
half a cauliflower, cut into florets
2 x 400g tins chopped tomatoes
200ml double cream
3 teaspoons curry powder
1 teaspoon ground ginger
6 teaspoons caster sugar
salt and black pepper
300g smoked skinless haddock
  fillets, cubed

300g skinless haddock
  fillets, cubed
500g skinless salmon
  fillets, cubed

for the topping
5 medium potatoes, peeled
  and cubed
4 sweet potatoes, peeled
  and cubed
125ml double cream
110g unsalted butter
1 teaspoon table salt

Sauté the onions in the vegetable oil in a large saucepan. When they begin to brown, add the aubergines and carrots, and a few minutes later add the cauliflower florets.

When the vegetables have softened, add the tinned tomatoes, double cream, spices, sugar, salt and pepper. Simmer for five minutes.

Add the fish and cook for ten minutes.

Next, make the topping. In a separate saucepan, cover the potatoes and sweet potatoes with water, bring to the boil, then reduce the heat and simmer until the vegetables are very soft.

Remove from the heat and drain.

Preheat the oven to 170°C/325°F/gas mark 3.

Add the cream, butter and salt, then mash well.

Place the fish mixture in an ovenproof dish (I use a casserole saucepan, which I can just transfer from hob to oven).

Add the topping and cook in the preheated oven for 15 to 20 minutes, until bubbling.

A Jewish Princess alternative to oysters and Champagne.

sweet and sour halibut

serves 4

4 halibut fillets
1 onion
3 bay leaves
salt and pepper

4 medium eggs
2 lemons squeezed
5 dessertspoons caster sugar
cucumber, for decoration

Place the fish in a saucepan along with the onion, bay leaves, salt and pepper. Cover with water and bring to the boil.

Simmer for 15 minutes.

When the fish is flaky, take 225ml of the stock out and strain into a bowl. Allow to cool.

Carefully take out the fish and place in a deep, heatproof glass dish.

Beat the eggs and squeeze the two lemons into the egg mixture.

Put this on a low heat, and slowly add the fish stock and sugar to taste.

When the mixture has thickened, pour it over the cooled fish.

Slice a cucumber thinly and use to decorate the dish.

This vintage recipe is like a good Gucci bag – it will never go out of date.

thai tuna

serves 4

4 large, fresh tuna steaks
juice of 2 limes
1 bunch of coriander,
  finely chopped
1 bunch of flat-leaf parsley,
  finely chopped
1 teaspoon lemon-grass purée
  (available in most
  good supermarkets)
½ teaspoon garlic purée

half a green chilli, chopped
  (if you like it hot, just use
  a whole chilli)
half a red pepper, finely chopped
6 cherry tomatoes,
  cut into quarters
rock salt and black pepper
  to season
olive oil

Place the tuna in a large bowl.

Squeeze on the lime juice, then add the rest of the ingredients and season to taste with salt and black pepper.

Leave to marinate for one hour.

Coat a griddle or frying pan with olive oil, heat, then add the tuna and sear each side.

Great for a girly lunch – especially if your friends are doing no carbs!

weights and measures

A Jewish Princess loves looking good. When you are thin, slim – whatever you want to call it – you're able to choose any jeans you want. If you're not lucky enough to be born with the skinny gene, then as every Princess knows, you've just got to work at it.

You can always try a tapeworm (I've heard of a supplier), or knock back a concoction of dubious herbal pills, hard-core drugs, colonic irrigation, and, as a last resort, liposuction. I've even heard of people trying to *think* themselves thin, but whenever I think of that four-letter word 'diet', I just think 'food'.

However, just like when choosing a handbag, when it comes to eating, I am *selective*. In restaurants I have been known to throw my fork down in disgust at some overly sweet or gelatinous dessert, but for fabulous food I am prepared to throw calorie caution to the wind.

Some Princesses may be in denial, but we all know that the only way to fit into those designer dresses is EXERCISE. Whether running round the shops, hitting the gym, or trying to swim with your head two feet above water (to protect your hair, of course), MOVING (yourself, that is, not changing your address) is the key to keeping your body from going south.

However, I love my food, and I am prepared to exercise my body so that I can exercise my mouth. From the number of other JPs I bump into at the gym, they've discovered this secret, too. Truth be known, I actually *love* exercise, from spinning to stepping, dancing to Pilates, you will find me doing my thaang! I find that all forms of exercise – and I mean *all* forms (except housework) – provide wonderful therapy. Exercise clears the mind, clears the cellulite and clears away the guilt that rears its ugly head whenever my fork finds that cheesecake.

All this talk of exercise has made me build up quite an appetite, so what better subject to talk about now than delicious desserts? Before we start, though, I think we should finish with one last exercise: flex your fingers and turn over the page...

7

desserts

desserts to die-t for!

I think everyone has a dessert they adore, a dessert they cannot turn down. If my son, for example, just so much as sniffs my Choca-challah Pudding (*see* page 134) baking in the oven, I'll find him prowling around the kitchen, waiting. *Challah* is delicious doughy bread made from eggs and is traditionally eaten on a Friday night. However, if there's any left over, my son gives me that puppy-dog look and I know that I will once again be whisking up eggs, chocolate and cream to make his favourite.

My own weakness is for ice cream. I just love it! I even get pleasure merely from *thinking* about it, and I get quite excited about a new special flavour. Ice cream has this unique smooth, cold, soft, melting texture that is amazing – and because it is so naughty, it is *soooooo* nice.

My relationship with ice cream once landed me in a spot of trouble.

I was entertaining some rather important clients and, due to nerves, had polished off a little too much of the pink stuff. When it came to dessert, I tottered in (high, high stilettos, naturally) with my magnificent tower of different-flavoured ice cream served in a giant brandy basket. One new, exciting flavour I had conjured up was Honey Halva Ice Cream (*see* page 138). *Halva* is a Middle Eastern delicacy made from sesame seeds which has a wonderful ability to stick to the roof of your mouth. Its unusual flavour combined with honey and made into ice cream is a winner. So it's no wonder that, in my eagerness to dive into my own dessert, I didn't wait a second before trying to serve it – and consequently could not prise the balls apart. Up shot a golden ball into the air and landed in the client's lap. I rushed over to help and found myself fumbling in said client's crotch. Scooping up the ball, I held it aloft like a triumphant egg-and-spoon-race winner and served it to his wife, who ate it. Oh dear!

Life is short. If you eat too much ice cream, life will be shorter. However, if you strike the right balance of 'moderation in everything', as my grandpa used to say, then indulging in your dessert fantasies should be encouraged, especially if it's a dessert to DIE-T for!

baked alaska

serves 6

1 box trifle sponges
marsala wine or brandy
the whites of 4 large eggs
225g caster sugar

1 x 450g carton vanilla
  ice cream
25g flaked almonds

Preheat the oven to 200°C/400°F/gas mark 6.

Place the sponges in an ovenproof dish and sprinkle with the Marsala or brandy.

Whisk the egg whites until stiff and add the sugar, whisking until the mixture is glossy.

Take the vanilla ice cream out of the freezer and leave it to soften slightly.

Smooth the ice cream over the sponges.

Spread the meringue mixture over the ice cream until it is completely covered.

If preferred, sprinkle the whole thing with flaked almonds and immediately place in the preheated oven for 20 minutes, or until the meringue mixture is lightly brown.

Serve immediately.

A great combination of cold and hot, this dessert will transport you to those snowy peaks.

black forest chocolate roulade

serves 6

1 x 435g tin black pitted
  cherries in syrup, drained
kirsh or cherry brandy
175g plain chocolate (use the
  type that contains 70% cocoa)

5 large eggs, separated
175g caster sugar
450ml double cream or non-dairy
  cream, whisked
icing sugar

The night before making the roulade, place the drained cherries in a bowl covered with your chosen liqueur and refrigerate.

Preheat the oven to 180°C/350°F/gas mark 4.

Melt the chocolate by putting it in a glass bowl over a saucepan filled with hot water.

Put the egg yolks and sugar in a mixing bowl and beat until pale. Add the melted chocolate. Beat until the mixture is smooth. Whisk the egg whites and fold into the mixture.

Pour into a Swiss roll tin lined with baking parchment that overlaps the side. Bake in the preheated oven for 15 to 20 minutes. Take out of the oven and leave to cool. Turn out onto greaseproof paper that has been dusted with icing sugar.

Whisk the cream and spread over the roulade. Drain the cherries, reserving the liqueur. With a hand blender, purée the cherries, then spread the purée over the cream.

Roll up the roulade; use the greaseproof paper, which is underneath, to help you. Place on a serving dish and decorate with icing sugar. Pour the reserved cherry liqueur in a jug to use when serving.

The seventies' dish reinvented. Very retro!

bread and butter pudding

serves 6

soft unsalted butter
orange marmalade
16 slices thick white bread,
   crusts removed
25g sultanas
3 large eggs

300ml milk
300ml whipping cream
110g caster sugar
grated rind of 1 orange
1 tablespoon demerara sugar

Preheat the oven to 180°C/350°F/gas mark 4.

Grease a 25cm ovenproof dish.

Spread the butter and marmalade on the bread and make a sandwich. Then butter the top of each sandwich.

After you have done all your sandwiches, cut them in two diagonally to create triangles.

Layer the triangles in the dish. Sprinkle on the sultanas.

In a separate bowl, whisk together the eggs, milk, cream and sugar. Pour over the triangles.

Grate the rind of the orange over the top and sprinkle on the demerara sugar.

Put the ovenproof dish inside a large roasting dish half-filled with water and place in the middle of the preheated oven. Bake for 30 minutes.

This should be served hot with cream or custard – fantastic as a real carb blow-out!

caramel ice cream

serves 6

8 tablespoons granulated sugar   600ml non-dairy cream
4 large egg yolks

In a saucepan, combine the sugar with four tablespoons of water and stir over a moderate heat until the sugar has dissolved completely. Let the sugar boil, swirling the pan occasionally until the sugar turns a light-brown colour.

Pour eight tablespoons of water into the caramel and simmer, stirring until it has melted.

Beat the egg yolks. Pour the syrup into them and continue beating until the mixture thickens.

Whisk the cream and fold into the mixture.

Pour the ice cream into a freezer-proof container and place in the freezer to set.

Try freezing the ice cream in a kugelhopf tin. When you turn it out, you'll have a hole in the middle, which you can then fill with various fruits.

cheater's cheese blintzes

serves 12

for the pancakes
(to cheat even more,
   just some buy ready-made!)
250g plain flour
2 large eggs
570ml full-fat milk
grated rind of 1 lemon
4 tablespoons oil, for frying

50g unsalted butter, to brush
   over the blintzes

for the filling
500g cream cheese
   (I use light)
6 tablespoons sour cream
2 large egg yolks
3 tablespoons caster sugar
1 teaspoon vanilla essence
50g sultanas
pinch of salt

to serve
sour cream, cherry jam or
   apple sauce

Mix all the pancake ingredients, except the oil, in a blender and leave in fridge for at least half an hour, or even better, overnight. When the above mixture is ready, make the filling simply by mixing together all the filling ingredients.

Whisk the batter before using to ensure a good consistency; you can easily do this with a hand whisk.

Coat a 20cm round, thin frying pan by pouring the oil onto it and swirling it around the pan, then pouring out any excess and wiping around the pan with a paper towel.

Heat the coated frying pan and pour on a thin layer of batter.

The pancake is ready when the mixture starts to bubble or comes away from the sides, so when that happens, just flip it over to lightly brown it. The first pancake is always a disaster, so don't worry – just eat it!

Turn the pancakes out onto a baking sheet. Continue this method, but keep oiling the pan after every two pancakes. Just stack the pancakes one on top of the other and leave to cool.

You should make approximately a dozen.

the blintz
Preheat the oven to 190°C/375°F/gas mark 5.

Take one pancake and fill it with the mixture, roll up the pancake, fold its sides and place in an ovenproof dish. Continue to do so with the others until the dish is filled.

Melt 50g unsalted butter and brush over the blintzes.

Bake in the preheated oven for 20 minutes, or until lightly browned.

Blintzes are delicious served warm with sour cream, cherry jam or apple sauce – or all three if you desire! If you're in a rush, just buy ready-made pancakes; they work equally well.

choca-challah pudding

serves 6

unsalted butter, for greasing
8 slices of a large *challah*
   1.5cm thick (one day old)
200g dark chocolate
   (the 70% cocoa type)
200ml double cream
300ml skimmed milk

115g unsalted butter
150g caster sugar
4 medium eggs

for decoration
icing sugar

Butter a medium ovenproof dish (I always use an oval one that's 35cm x 24cm x 6cm).

Remove the crusts from the *challah*. If the slices are very large, cut them in half.

Place the chocolate, cream, milk, butter and sugar into a double saucepan (bain-marie) over a low heat, stirring all the time, until the mixture is melted and smooth. If you haven't got a double saucepan, then just use a saucepan of boiling water with a heatproof bowl over it and put the ingredients in the bowl.

Remove the bowl from the heat and leave it to cool.

Beat the eggs and stir them slowly into the chocolate mixture.

Pour half the sauce into the bottom of the ovenproof dish.

Place the sliced *challah* into the liquid, pressing down with the back of a tablespoon to allow the bread to begin to saturate.

Pour over the remaining liquid and do this again to allow the sauce to saturate the bread and completely cover the *challah*.

Cover the dish and leave to cool, then refrigerate it for a minimum of two hours.

Preheat the oven to 180°C/350°F/gas mark 4.

Bake in a bain marie (I do this by putting the dish on a roasting tray and filling it with water until it reaches halfway up the outside of the dish) in the preheated oven for about 20 minutes.

Dust with icing sugar to decorate and serve warm.

A fantastic way of using leftover challah – and a wonderfully chocolicious dessert.

coffee and amaretti ice

serves 8

3 large eggs
55g caster sugar
300ml non-dairy cream

3 tablespoons coffee essence
200g amaretti biscuits

Whisk the eggs and sugar together until pale and creamy in colour, with a texture like whipped cream.

Add the non-dairy cream to the mixture and continue to whisk until thick.

Whisk in the coffee essence.

Bash the biscuits with a rolling pin to form broken pieces and fold these into the mixture.

Place the mixture into a container and leave overnight to freeze.

A gondola moment.

fruit brûlée

serves 6

seasonal fruits such as
  strawberries, raspberries
  or fresh peaches
600ml double cream

1 vanilla pod, split
4 large egg yolks
1 level tablespoon caster sugar
extra sugar, for the caramel

Make a fruit salad in advance and put it into an ovenproof dish.

To make the brûlée, put the cream and the vanilla pod into a double saucepan (bain-marie) over a moderate heat. (If you haven't got a double saucepan, use a saucepan of boiling water with a heatproof bowl over it and put the ingredients in the bowl.) Stir continuously and bring to scalding point.

Beat the four egg yolks thoroughly with the sugar.

Remove the vanilla pod from the cream and pour in the egg-yolk mixture. Turn down the heat and stir continuously for about five minutes, until the cream thickens. Keep a very beady eye on this tricky procedure; if the mixture boils, it will be ruined!

Pour this warm, thick mixture over the fruit salad. Cool. Place in the refrigerator for at least six hours (or better still, overnight) to set.

The next day, cover the brûlée evenly with about half a centimetre of caster sugar and place under a preheated very, very hot grill, turning the dish to allow the mixture to melt in order to caramelize. Make sure the top is evenly browned, then serve.

For this procedure, you can use a chef's blowtorch – but watch out for your nails!

honey halva ice cream

serves 8

3 large eggs
50g caster sugar
300ml non-dairy cream

225g *halva* – plain or any other
  flavour of your choice, crumbled
3 dessertspoons clear honey

Whisk the eggs and sugar until pale cream in colour, with a texture like whipped cream.

Whisk the cream until thick and then fold the crumbled *halva* into the cream.

Fold the egg mixture gently into the cream mixture, then drizzle in the honey and fold it in gently.

Put the mixture into an ice-cream bomb container (or any container suitable for freezing) and leave overnight in the freezer.

For those who have a sweet tooth, grab a spoon and indulge!

A Jewish Princess knows that
being happy keeps you young,
so I suggest a fabulous anti-ageing
cream. You can buy it everywhere,
it comes in huge pots, it's very
economical and it's always
available when you are feeling
a little down.

The name? Ice cream.
Just don't apply too much!

meringue malibu roulade

serves 6

5 large free-range egg whites
225g caster sugar
110g desiccated coconut
icing sugar, for dusting

225ml whisked non-dairy cream
(or the real mccoy)
1 tablespoon malibu
200g chopped pineapple

Preheat the oven to 160°C/325°F/gas mark 3.

Whisk the egg whites until stiff, then add the caster sugar. Whisk until the mixture forms thick peaks.

Fold in the desiccated coconut.

Line a roulade tin with baking paper.

Spoon the mixture onto the baking paper and spread it evenly with a spatula. Bake in the preheated oven for 30 minutes.

Cover with a damp teatowel and leave to cool for at least two hours; the teatowel keeps the cake from drying out.

Place a large sheet of baking paper on a kitchen surface and dust it with the icing sugar.

Whisk the cream with the Malibu.

Turn the roulade onto the baking paper and spread it with the Malibu cream.

Place the pineapple chunks all over the cream.

Take the ends of baking paper and start to roll. DO THIS ALONE
SO YOU DON'T FEEL PUT UNDER PRESSURE!

Place the roulade into an oblong dish and decorate with any
leftover pineapple.

*If cracks appear, don't worry – that's how it's supposed to look!
This is a surprisingly sophisticated desert, but easy to do and
well worth the effort.*

pecan pie

serves 6

225g shortcrust pastry
3 large eggs
175ml golden syrup
1 tablespoon grand marnier

pinch of salt
110g soft brown sugar
200g pecans, shelled

Preheat the oven to 180°C/350°F/gas mark 4.

Line a 22-24cm flan dish with the pastry.

Fill with baking beans and bake in the preheated oven for ten minutes.

Leave to cool and remove the beans.

Cream together the eggs, golden syrup and Grand Marnier.

Add the pinch of salt and brown sugar and mix well.

Fold in the pecans.

Pour the mixture into the pastry case and bake for 20 minutes, or until the filling has risen and turned light brown.

Serve warm or cold.

For extra calories, add a dollop of thick cream or vanilla ice cream.

shikerer's tipple

serves 6

2 litres vanilla ice cream
500g dried pitted
  prunes, chopped

110g sultanas
225ml brandy
75g plain chocolate drops

Soak the prunes and sultanas in the brandy for an hour.

Take the ice cream out of the freezer and allow it to thaw slightly.

Place the ice cream, prunes, sultanas and liqueur into a mixer
and blend well.

Stir in the chocolate drops.

Pour the ice-cream mixture into a freezer-proof serving dish, and
place in freezer to set.

This is a great accompaniment to any pudding or pie.

sticky briti pudding

serves 6-8

2 x 415g tins pears, in juice
  (reserve the juice of 1 tin)
65g unsalted butter
200g dark-brown sugar
2 large eggs
250g self-raising flour
125ml dark rum
1 teaspoon bicarbonate of soda

for the sauce
300ml double cream
200g dark-brown sugar
75g unsalted butter

Preheat the oven to 180°C/350°F/gas mark 4.

Butter a 20cm ovenproof dish. Put one tin of drained sliced pears at the bottom of dish.

In a large bowl, mix together the butter, sugar, eggs and flour.

Put the other tin of drained pears, the rum and 125ml pear juice in a saucepan and simmer for 4 minutes.

Remove from the heat and allow to cool.

Stir in the bicarbonate of soda.

Add the pear mixture to the butter mixture.

Pour into the ovenproof dish and bake for 30-40 minutes in the preheated oven.

Check that the pudding is cooked through by putting a knife in the middle; if it comes out clean, it's done.

To make the sauce, mix all the sauce ingredients in the saucepan and cook gently until the sugar has dissolved.

Make a few holes in the pudding with a knife or other sharp instrument.

Pour the sauce onto the pudding, allowing it to seep through, and serve.

You can double up the mixture and freeze one for a later date. Alternatively, put the sponge in the freezer and defrost when ready to use. You can then make the sauce while reheating the sponge, which will take 20 minutes in a hot oven. Then just pour on the sauce as described above.

summer fruit pavlova

serves 8

the whites of 4 large eggs
225g caster sugar
225ml double cream
  (or non-dairy version)

4 kiwi fruits, for decorating
  (or any other fruits in season)

Preheat the oven to 140°C/275°F/gas mark 1.

Make a template by drawing a soft pencil line around a large round plate on a baking sheet.

Whisk the egg whites until stiff and add the caster sugar slowly while still whisking. Carry on whisking until the mixture resembles stiff peaks.

Use a spatula and shape the mixture onto a baking sheet to form a round pavlova.

Bake in the preheated oven for about one hour 30 minutes, then switch off the heat and leave the pavlova to cool inside the oven – the longer, the better.

When ready to serve, whisk the cream and spread it over the pavlova, and decorate with the fruits of your choice.

You can change the fruits according to the season – a bit like your clothes.

ten-minute trifle

serves 8

2 shop-bought raspberry
  swiss rolls
1 small bowl filled with sherry
2 x 450g tins
  raspberries, drained
2 large handfuls of roasted
  flaked almonds

140g fresh sweet raspberries
450ml fresh thick custard
300ml double cream
all of the above ingredients are
  approximate – it really depends
  on the size of the bowl you are
  going to use

Slice the Swiss rolls and dip the pieces into the bowl of sherry
until the cake is saturated.

Line the bottom and sides of a glass dish with the Swiss roll.

Pour on the drained raspberries and a handful of almonds.

Next, add the fresh raspberries.

Pour the custard over the fruit.

Place in the fridge.

Whisk the cream.

Dry pan-fry the rest of the almonds until golden.

Spread the cream on top of trifle and sprinkle with the
toasted almonds.

*This may take only ten minutes to make, but your guests will
be impressed.*

tiramisu

serves 6

4 large eggs, separated
175g caster sugar
500g mascapone cheese
2 boxes boudoir biscuits
  (approximately 44 biscuits)

approximately 300ml marsala
approximately 2 tablespoons
  coffee essence
cocoa powder

Beat together the egg yolks and sugar, then add the cheese and beat until it forms a smooth, creamy mixture.

Whisk the egg whites until soft peaks form.

Slowly whisk the egg whites into the cheese mixture.

In a shallow bowl, pour in the wine and coffee essence.

Quickly dip a boudoir biscuit one at a time into the wine mixture and place at the bottom of a glass dish about 30cm x 20cm.

Place the biscuits next to each other to form a line of a single layer.

Pour a layer of the cheese mixture over these biscuits, then place a layer of quickly dipped biscuits over the cheese mixture, and finally pour on the remaining cheese mixture.

Sieve the cocoa powder over the top of the dessert and put it in the fridge to set.

The Jewish version of the Italian mama's cheesecake.

A waiter came to take the
table's dessert order.
The Jewish Princess fancied a
little bit of everything – so when
her turn came, she knew exactly
what to request:

'A fork, please!'

toffee apple pie

serves 8

for the base
75g melted unsalted butter
225g digestive biscuits, crushed
  (put the biscuits in a bag and
  bash them with a rolling pin)

for the toffee
400ml condensed milk
50g caster sugar
50g unsalted butter

for the filling
350g eating apples,
  peeled and quartered
1 tablespoon maple syrup

for the topping
300ml double cream,
  lightly whipped
1 crunchie bar

Mix the melted butter with the crushed biscuits.

Press into the base of a 21cm springform tin and chill for
ten minutes.

Put the condensed milk, sugar and butter in a non-stick saucepan.
Place the saucepan over a low heat, stirring constantly.

Once the butter has melted, increase the heat and bring the
mixture up to boiling point, stirring constantly, and lifting the
saucepan off the heat to stop the sauce from burning. The mixture
will thicken; this should take no longer than five minutes.

Pour the mixture over the base and return it to the fridge.

Place the apple pieces in a microwave-safe dish.

Cook on a high heat in the microwave for six minutes.

Halfway through, remove the dish from the microwave, stir the apples and then replace to ensure even cooking.

Drain and mix with the maple syrup.

Place the syrupy apples on top of the toffee and put the pie back in the fridge.

Whisk the cream and spread it on top of the pie, then decorate with broken pieces of the Crunchie bar.

To ensure the toffee apple pie stays in one piece, use a sharp knife and run it around the edge of the tin before removing it.

8

cakes

cakes just like grandma made

My grandmother made unbelievable cakes. Her cakes were actually legendary, and to this day my friends still reminisce about the after-school tea parties we had.

Whenever she used to visit, she always arrived with pallets and pallets of farm-laid eggs, crates and crates of fruit and other bulk purchases from the cash-and-carry. I think this bulk-buying habit was due to the war years and her fear of not having enough food. My mother and I seem to have followed suit and are always overstocking our fridges and freezers ('just in case').

Grandma would spend her visits glued to the food mixer in the kitchen, baking and baking – and of course I liked nothing better than to spend time with her, helping, licking the bowl, watching and sniffing the delicious aroma of *cake*.

I have to confess that I was a social saddo in my early teens; yes, even Jewish Princesses can have some 'backward' years! My social life was practically nil. While my friends had boyfriends and were partying their nights away, my family had moved – and we were, as far as I was concerned, too far from civilization. My Saturday nights were spent, I'm almost ashamed to say, *baking*.

I realize now, however, just how incredibly therapeutic baking is. I am sure my grandma used to bake so much to get over the loss of my beloved grandpa. I, in turn, baked so much to cope with yearning for my knight in shining armour to turn up on his white charger. Amazingly, he eventually did turn up: not 'on', but 'in' a white Honda Prelude – nearly Princess Perfect!

So forget yoga or Pilates; baking is an incredible way to escape your troubles and get lost in a world of flour, eggs and sugar. To see such basic ingredients transformed into treats as wonderful as the cakes in this chapter is always a truly satisfying experience.

almond cake

225g softened unsalted butter
175g caster sugar
4 medium eggs, separated
1 pinch of salt
175g self-raising flour
50g ground almonds
1 teaspoon baking powder
1 teaspoon almond essence

for the icing
approximately 2 tablespoons
   boiling water
225g icing sugar
25g flaked almonds

Preheat the oven to 160°C/325°F/gas mark 3.

Cream the butter and sugar until pale.

In another bowl, whisk the egg whites until they form soft peaks (add a pinch of salt).

Mix the self-raising flour with the ground almonds and baking powder.

Add the dry ingredients to the creamed butter and sugar.

Slowly add the egg yolks and almond essence.

Fold in the egg whites.

Line or grease a loose-bottomed 21cm tin.

Bake in the preheated oven for 35 to 40 minutes.

Cool before turning out onto a wire rack.

To make the icing, slowly stir the boiling water into the icing sugar.

Place the icing in a double bowl (bain-marie) and, on a low heat, keep stirring until the sugar has melted and the icing is easy to spread. (If you don't have a bain-marie, place the ingredients in a bowl and put this over a pan of boiling water.)

Heat a frying pan and dry-fry the flaked almonds.

Once you've iced the cake, decorate it with the toasted almonds.

Don't feel too guilty when eating this treat, as almonds are great for the skin!

anytime cake

225g unsalted butter
225g caster sugar
4 medium eggs
1 teaspoon vanilla essence
225g self-raising flour

optional extras
110g sultanas
or 110g chocolate chips
or 110g glacé cherries…
  or all three!

Preheat the oven to 180°C/350°F/gas mark 4.

Cream the butter and sugar, then add the rest of the ingredients – and then add an optional extra to make it into the cake you fancy to break your diet on!

Pour the batter into a greased 21cm baking tin.

Bake in the preheated oven for 45 minutes to an hour, testing with a knife to see if it has cooked through.

The cake mixture can also be divided into muffin cases. Bake them for ten minutes, then decorate with icing sugar and sweets for fairy cakes.

apple brûlée cake

450g eating apples,
  peeled and sliced
110g self-raising flour
1 teaspoon baking powder
110g caster sugar
6 tablespoons milk
4 tablespoons unsalted
  butter, melted
2 medium eggs
1 teaspoon cinnamon

for the topping
75g unsalted butter, softened
110g caster sugar
1 teaspoon vanilla essence
1 egg

Preheat the oven to 160°C/325°F/gas mark 3.

Put the thinly sliced apples into the base of a greased and floured 21cm loose-bottomed tin.

Put the rest of the cake ingredients into the bowl and beat until smooth.

Pour the batter over the apples, spreading it evenly, and bake in the preheated oven for 30 to 40 minutes, or until lightly golden.

Meanwhile, cream the topping ingredients.

Remove the cake from the oven and spoon over the topping.

Bake for a further 20 to 25 minutes, until the topping is a golden brown.

This cake is delicious served hot or cold. The way to my husband's heart is with this cake – but he's taken!

as sweet as channie 'honey' cake

450g self-raising flour
225g caster sugar
grated rind and juice of
   1 large orange
1 teaspoon mixed spice
1 teaspoon cinnamon

½ teaspoon bicarbonate of soda
225ml corn oil
3 medium eggs
450ml golden syrup
225ml boiled water
flaked almonds, for decorating

Preheat the oven to 180°C/350°F/gas mark 4.

Sieve the flour.

In a bowl, mix all dry ingredients together – *i.e.* flour, sugar, orange rind, mixed spice, cinnamon, bicarbonate of soda.

Combine all the wet ingredients in another bowl then add them to the dry ingredients. Mix together.

Pour the mixture into a 25cm square cake tin and decorate with flaked almonds if desired.

Bake in the preheated oven for 50 to 60 minutes, always checking towards the end.

Even though there is no honey in this cake, it is still considered 'honey' cake by JPs. Honey cake is always made for the Jewish New Year to wish friends and family sweet success for the coming year. This one is delicious served warm, sliced and buttered.

banana cake

225g softened unsalted butter
250g caster sugar
2 large egg yolks
225g plain flour
1 teaspoon baking powder

½ teaspoon salt
4 tablespoons sour cream
2 medium-sized ripe bananas
1 teaspoon vanilla essence
5 large egg whites, whisked

Preheat the oven to 180°C/350°F/gas mark 4.

Mix the butter and sugar together.

Add the egg yolks to the mixture and continue to beat.

Add the flour, baking powder, salt, sour cream, bananas and vanilla and blend well.

Fold in the whisked egg whites.

Pour the batter into a greased 20cm square tin and bake in the preheated oven for 45 minutes.

This is great served warm with butter. Even if people don't like bananas, they will be surprised at how delicious this recipe is.

a word about cheesecake

There are many reasons why I love making cheesecake.

1   It's a fantastic stress release when you bash the hell out of those biscuits (are your children getting on your nerves?), plus it's quite a good arm workout.

2   It usually qualifies for the fewer-than-ten-ingredients rule.

3   It always comes out of the oven completely level, so it looks highly professional.

4   It takes ten minutes to prepare and 30 minutes to cook so I can still go to my Sunday spinning class.

5   What really encouraged me in my baking of cheesecake was when I gave a cheesecake to one of my husband's clients (very, very famous artists) and they said (just wait for this – it's very exciting and great for my Princess ego) that it was: 'The BEST cheesecake they had ever tasted.'

Do you think if I made them enough cheesecake they would give me a 'piece' of their work?

Every Jewish Princess knows
that cakes have no calories if you:
* take a bite from somebody
   else's plate;
* stand on one leg when eating;
* sniff them;
* only eat the top;
* only eat the bottom;
* only ever nibble a sliver!

If you're suffering with PMT
(Princess Menstrual Tension),
of course, then anything goes!

peanut butter cheesecake

8 digestive biscuits
2 tablespoons smooth
  peanut butter
1 tablespoon unsalted butter
175g caster sugar
4 medium eggs
450g curd cheese
2 tablespoons sour cream

peanut butter topping
3 tablespoons smooth
  peanut butter
2 tablespoons sour cream
1 tablespoon single cream
caster sugar to taste
a handful of crushed
  salted peanuts

Preheat the oven to 150°C/300°F/gas mark 2.

Crush the biscuits by putting them into a bag and bashing them with a rolling pin.

In a small saucepan, melt the peanut butter and butter, then add the crushed biscuits and mix well.

In a greased, round springform tin, approximately 21cm in diameter, press the biscuit mixture down to form the base.

Beat together the sugar and eggs until the mixture is light and frothy.

Add the curd cheese and sour cream.

Cook for approximately 20 minutes in the preheated oven, or until the edges are firm but the middle is slightly wobbly.

Turn off the oven and let the cake cool inside with the door slightly open.

When cold, refrigerate it for at least two to three hours.

To make the topping, melt the peanut butter in a saucepan on a low heat, then add the sour cream and the single cream – DO NOT let the mixture boil!

As soon as these ingredients are stirred in, remove from the heat and add enough sugar to suit your own taste.

When the topping is cool, remove the cheesecake from the fridge and spread the peanut butter topping on top.

Garnish with a handful of crushed salted peanuts.

If you like peanut butter, this cheesecake is orgasmic!

the ultimate cheesecake

for the base
450g digestive
   biscuits, crushed
1 teaspoon cinnamon
110g melted
   unsalted butter
75g caster sugar

for the cake
75g sultanas
2 large eggs
3 tablespoons milk
550g cream cheese
75g caster sugar
1 teaspoon
   vanilla essence

for the topping
300ml sour cream
1 teaspoon
   vanilla essence
2 tablespoons
   caster sugar

for decoration
fresh fruit

Preheat the oven to 180°C/350°F/gas mark 4.

To make the base, mix together the base ingredients, making sure the biscuits are well-crushed, and press into a 23cm to 25cm springform tin. Use a fork to press the mixture down on the base and up around the sides until the tin is well-covered.

Bake in the preheated oven for ten minutes.

Cool, then sprinkle the sultanas over the bottom.

Mix together the rest of the ingredients, pour on top of the base and bake for 30 minutes.

Remove the cheesecake from the oven and allow it to cool for 15 minutes.

Meanwhile, make the topping by mixing all the topping ingredients together.

Pour over the cheesecake, return it to the oven and bake for a further ten minutes. Leave to cool.

Refrigerate overnight.

Pile fresh fruit such as strawberries and blueberries on top of this cheesecake. It gives it a great look and tastes delicious.

carrot cake

100g self-raising flour
1 teaspoon baking powder
½ teaspoon cinnamon
1 pinch salt
200g light brown sugar
15g olive oil
2 medium eggs
200g carrots, grated
150g ground almonds

for the frosting
175g light cream cheese
55g icing sugar
25g softened unsalted butter

for decoration
a handful of toasted pine nuts

Preheat the oven to 170°C/325°F/gas mark 3.

Sieve and mix together the flour, baking powder, cinnamon and salt.

Add the brown sugar, olive oil and eggs and mix well.

Mix in the carrots and ground almonds.

Put the mixture into a greased 20cm cake tin and bake in the preheated oven for 30 minutes.

Turn the cake out onto a wire rack and leave it to cool.

To make the frosting, use a hand blender to mix all ingredients together in a bowl until smooth.

When the cake is cold, spread the frosting on top.

Decorate with toasted pine nuts, if desired.

A cake full of vitamins that can be used to improve your suntan if eaten regularly!

chocolate refrigerator cake

225g plain chocolate
2 large eggs
2 level dessertspoons caster sugar
225g melted unsalted butter
225g plain digestive
  biscuits, crushed
110g salted peanuts

75g chopped walnuts
225g glacé cherries, chopped
1 teaspoon vanilla essence
a handful of walnut halves,
  for decoration

Break the chocolate into squares and place in a double-saucepan (bain-marie) or in a small bowl over a pan of hot water to melt.

Beat the eggs and sugar together, then beat in the melted butter.

Stir in the chocolate and fold in the broken biscuits, together with the nuts, glacé cherries and vanilla essence.

Pour the mixture into a buttered Pyrex dish 15cm to 18cm deep and leave in the fridge to set for at least six hours.

When ready to turn out, use a sharp knife and run it around the edges of the cake. Immerse the dish halfway in hot water to allow the cake to melt a bit and then turn it out.

Decorate with the walnuts and refrigerate until ready to use.

When serving, cut into small slices as this cake is very rich. Delicious used as a petite four with coffee.

de luxe chocolate cake

175g dark chocolate
  (the 70% cocoa type)
110g softened unsalted butter
1 tablespoon grand marnier
5 medium eggs, separated
110g ground almonds
1 pinch of salt

75g caster sugar
2 tablespoons double cream

for the raspberry glaze
4 tablespoons raspberry jam
  (with seeds)
1 tablespoon caster sugar

Preheat the oven to 170°C/325°F/gas mark 3.

Melt the chocolate and butter in a double saucepan (bain-marie), stirring constantly so that the mixture does not burn. If you haven't got a double saucepan, then just use a saucepan of boiling water with a heatproof bowl over it and put the ingredients in the bowl.

Let the chocolate mixture cool. You can speed this up by standing the bowl in cold water.

Stir in the Grand Marnier, egg yolks and ground almonds.

In a separate bowl, whisk the egg whites with a pinch of salt until soft peaks form, then slowly add the sugar.

Gently fold the egg whites into the chocolate mixture.

Add the cream and gently fold it into the mixture.

Pour into a greased and floured 20cm springform tin.

Place in the centre of the preheated oven for 25 minutes, or until a knife stuck in the middle comes out clean.

When the cake has cooled, release it and place it on a serving dish.

When the you are ready to glaze, place the raspberry jam and sugar in a saucepan and heat gently, stirring so that the glaze does not burn. When the mixture becomes syrupy, remove it from the heat.

Pour the glaze over the top and let it run down the sides.

Even when this cake is served as a dessert after a large meal, there is never any left over! If you don't like raspberry jam, simply try making the glaze with the jam of your choice.

english fruit cake with a cup of tea

250g mixed chopped
  dried fruit
grated rind of
  1 whole orange
4 english breakfast tea bags
600ml hot water
3 large eggs
110g caster sugar
110g softened unsalted butter
2 tablespoons milk

280g self-raising flour,
  plus 3 tablespoons
1 teaspoon baking powder

for decoration
1 handful of blanched almonds
1 tablespoon demerara sugar

Preheat the oven to 150°C/300°F/gas mark 2.

In a large heatproof bowl, place the dried fruit and orange rind.

Make a pot of tea with the four tea bags and boiling water and leave it to brew.

Pour the tea over the fruit until it is just covered and leave to marinate for a couple of hours.

Whisk the eggs and sugar together until the mixture has expanded and is nice and frothy.

Add the butter slowly, in small pieces.

Strain the fruit, reserving the tea, and dry it on kitchen paper, then lightly dust it with the three tablespoons of flour.

With the mixer set on slow, add the fruit, milk and the reserved tea to the egg, sugar and butter mixture.

Sift together the self-raising flour and the baking powder, then add this to the cake mixture.

Grease and flour a 20cm springform tin and pour in the batter.

Decorate with a handful of blanched almonds and sugar.

Bake in the preheated oven for 55 to 60 minutes.

A very useful aprés-school-run cake. This is best made the day before serving.

grandpa's favourite coffee and walnut cake

225g unsalted butter
225g caster sugar
4 large eggs
110g chopped walnuts
2 tablespoons coffee essence
225g self-raising flour
2 teaspoons baking powder

for the icing
175g unsalted butter
450g sifted icing sugar
4 tablespoons milk
6 teaspoons coffee essence

for decoration
walnut halves and coffee beans

Preheat the oven to 160°C/325°F/gas mark 3.

Mix all the cake ingredients together and divide into two greased 18cm baking tins.

Bake in the preheated oven for 25 to 30 minutes, checking that the sponges are baked by putting a skewer in. If it comes out clean, they're done.

Remove the cakes from the oven and leave them to cool.

Make the icing by combining all the ingredients, then use some of it to sandwich the sponges together.

Ice the cake all over, and decorate with walnut pieces interspersed with coffee beans.

The best present for Grandpa on birthdays, anniversaries or any occasion.

honey cake

225g plain flour
115g caster sugar
1 teaspoon cinnamon
1 teaspoon mixed spice
50g clear honey
115ml golden syrup

50ml cooking oil
2 medium eggs
1 teaspoon bicarbonate
  of soda
80ml smooth orange juice

Preheat the oven to 170°C/325°F/gas mark 3.

Grease and flour a 20cm cake tin.

In a large bowl, mix together the flour, sugar and spices.

Add the honey, syrup, oil and eggs.

Beat well until smooth.

Use another large bowl and dissolve the bicarbonate of soda
in the orange juice. Stir well (this will fizz) and then add this to
the mixture.

Bake in the preheated oven for 40 to 60 minutes.

It is a good idea to make this cake the day before eating.
As it matures, it becomes even more syrupy and delicious.

marble cake

3 large eggs, separated
175g unsalted butter
200g caster sugar
1 teaspoon vanilla essence
225g self-raising flour
3 tablespoons milk

75g plain chocolate drops
(or milk chocolate, if you prefer)
4 tablespoons plain chocolate
spread (or milk chocolate,
if you prefer)

Preheat the oven to 180°C/350°F/gas mark 4.

Whisk the egg whites until stiff. Leave them in the bowl and put to one side for later.

In a separate bowl, beat the egg yolks, vanilla essence and butter until creamy. Add the sugar gradually, beating until the mixture resembles whipped cream.

Now comes the tricky part. Keep the mixer going on low and add to it a tablespoon of flour and alternate with a tablespoon of milk and a tablespoon of the egg whites that you whisked at the beginning. Keep doing this until all the ingredients have been used. (This is a bit of a pain, but really worth doing as it makes the cake very light.)

Divide the mixture into two. Place one half into a new bowl and add the chocolate drops to it.

Pour the mixture containing the chocolate drops into a greased 20cm baking tin and spread it out over the bottom.

Add the chocolate spread to the other half of the mixture and mix well. Pour this over the chocolate-drop mixture in the baking tin.

By making a figure of eight with a spatula, swirl the dark chocolate-spread mixture gently through the chocolate-drop mixture, so that you get a marbling effect. When you do this, lift the spatula upwards to allow the white mixture to come to the top.

Smooth the top of the mixture and bake for 45 to 60 minutes.

I can remember fighting with my brother as to whose turn it was to lick the bowl when we were children. Sometimes for children (and even a few adults!) this cake mixture is even more delicious than the finished cake. So leave the bowl for the kids – or if they're at school, add washing up liquid and quickly fill it with water to prevent you from licking.

marmalade cream cake

175g softened unsalted butter,
  cut into small pieces
175g caster sugar
3 medium eggs
1 teaspoon
  orange-flower water
3 tablespoons full-fat milk
1 tablespoon warm water
175g fine self-raising flour
2 teaspoons baking powder

for the marmalade-cream filling
300ml whipping cream
3 tablespoons orange
  marmalade (thin-cut)

for decoration
icing sugar
grated rind of 1 whole orange

Preheat the oven to 160°C/325°F/gas mark 3.

Grease and flour two 20cm sandwich tins.

In a large bowl, cream the butter and sugar together until pale.

Add the eggs, one at a time, beating after each addition.

Add the orange-flower water, and beat it in.

Mix the milk with the warm water, then add to the mixture and continue to beat.

Add all the dry ingredients and mix thoroughly.

Pour into the prepared sandwich tins and bake in the preheated oven for approximately 20 minutes.

Once the cake has cooled, turn it out onto a wire rack.

To make the filling, whisk the whipping cream until firm.

Stir the marmalade so that it is loosened up and soft, then add it gently to the whipped cream.

Fill the centre of the cake with the marmalade cream.

To decorate, grate the orange over the top of the cake and then lightly dust with icing sugar.

This is a wonderful cake to serve for a Sunday tea.

sour cream cake

75g unsalted butter
1 teaspoon cinnamon
175g (approximately 14)
  digestive biscuits, crushed
425ml sour cream

110g caster sugar
1 medium egg
1 x 110g tin raspberries, drained
fresh raspberries, for decoration
more sour cream, for serving

Preheat the oven to 150°C/300°F/gas mark 2.

Grease a 22cm springform cake tin.

Melt the butter in a saucepan over a gentle heat. Add the cinnamon, stir, then add the cinnamon-butter to the crushed biscuits in a large bowl.

Press the mixture into the bottom of the baking tin to make a base.

Bake in the preheated oven for five minutes.

Whisk together the sour cream, sugar and egg.

Add the well-drained tinned raspberries.

Pour the sour cream mixture over the base and bake for 40 minutes, or until set.

Remove the cake from the oven. When cool, refrigerate it in the tin for at least an hour to allow it to set.

Remove the cake from tin right before serving.

Decorate with fresh raspberries and serve with a little sour cream on the side.

Be warned: one slice is never enough!

whisky cake

finely grated rind of
  1 large orange
4 tablespoons whisky
175g sultanas

175g unsalted butter
175g caster sugar
3 large eggs
225g self-raising flour

Soak the grated orange rind in the whisky for at least an hour, then add the sultanas and soak for a further 45 minutes.

Preheat the oven to 180°C/350°F/gas mark 4.

Grease and line a 20cm round cake tin with baking parchment.

In a large bowl, cream together the butter and sugar until light in colour, then add the eggs.

Fold in the flour.

Add the sultanas and whisky mixture.

Pour the batter into the prepared tin and bake in the middle of the preheated oven for one hour.

Cool completely before turning out and serving.

When the nights are drawing in, a slice of this is great with a cup of tea.

zesty lemon cake

4 medium eggs
225g caster sugar
225g softened unsalted butter
2 tablespoons milk
1 1/2 teaspoons
   lemon essence
grated rind of
   1 whole lemon
225g self-raising flour
1 teaspoon baking powder

for the lemon syrup
juice of 2 lemons
grated rind of
   1 lemon
grated rind of
   1 orange
6 tablespoons water
16 tablespoons caster sugar

Preheat the oven to 180°C/350°F/gas mark 4.

In a large bowl, whisk the eggs with the sugar until the mixture is frothy and the sugar is fully dissolved.

Add the softened butter, slowly, in small pieces.

Add the milk and lemon essence.

In another bowl, mix the rind of one whole lemon with the flour and baking powder, then add this to the egg mixture.

Pour the mixture into a greased and floured 20cm x 20cm square springform tin.

Place the tin in the middle of the preheated oven and bake for 45 minutes.

To make the syrup, place all of the syrup ingredients in a saucepan.

Bring to boiling point and keep it there for at least three minutes, sitrring constantly, until the syrup has gone a golden colour.

As the cake comes out of the oven, prick it all over and pour the syrup over the top. It looks lovely with the mixture of lemon and orange rind.

When the cake is cool, lift it out of the tin.

This cake is a combination of sweet and sharp, chewy and spongy – and absolutely delicious!

9

the ultimate dinner

the ultimate friday night dinner

Friday night. The Sabbath or *Shabbos*. The night the family sits down together to share a wonderful meal. This is the night when the house is filled with incredible smells of cooking. The smell of chicken soup permeates every room.

The table is laid with a crisp, white tablecloth. The *Shabbos* candles sit in their treasured silver candlesticks. The gleaming silver *kiddush* cup filled with *kiddush* wine is ready for the blessing, and two wonderful freshly baked *challas* sit side by side, covered with a beautifully embroidered cloth.

This is the night when we reconnect with our spiritual being and are thankful for the week and the Sabbath still to come. For Jews, the Friday night dinner is a bit like Christmas – except instead of having to make this feast once a year, we have the blessing of making it once a week! The Friday night dinner fantasy is one of Father returning home from work in plenty of time before sundown, bearing flowers for his beautiful wife. The children are in their best clothes, faces shining like little angels, while Mother makes the blessing over the candles, looking like she has taken a break from the film set of *Fiddler on the Roof*. The house is serene, the conversation around the table jovial, interesting and happy.

Unfortunately, I have since discovered that the fantasy of the Sabbath meal is, of course, nothing like reality.

Reality is: Husband returns home from work very, very late and flowerless. Your teenager has to be prised off the phone and strapped into her seat at the table, while the younger children, stuck with masses of homework, are moody and tired from a long week of school. Mother is – well, of course being a JP, *she's* perfect! But as far as the conversation around the table goes, if you're not careful, it can wind up turning into World War III.

Over the years, I have found ways of dealing with Friday night dinners and ways of turning the reality into at least a little bit of the fantasy. Firstly, I always try to invite guests over. On the face of it, this seems insane, but like most things in my life, there is method in my madness. Even though I now have more work to do, there are many advantages. For one thing, my husband magically gets home on time (even if he shoots in just before the guests arrive) – and sometimes he's even bearing flowers.

The teenager looks respectable and manages to unglue the phone from her ear (even teenagers have a social conscience).

The younger children are excited that guests are coming over and even enjoy showing off by helping to clear up.

Guests always lighten the atmosphere, too, so there are never any arguments around the table – plus they are actually *grateful* for my culinary delights. An additional bonus is that we invariably get invited back, so there's one less Friday night dinner for me to do.

I have also learned to prepare the Friday night dinner early. Chicken soup is cooked on Wednesday, the table is laid and desserts made on Thursday, and on Friday I only allow one hour to prepare the rest of the food.

One hour may seem a short amount of time to prepare this feast, but as I have learned, you can prepare the same amount of food in one hour that used to take you days. It's just a matter of self-belief – and making things simple.

If, one week, you are too tired or too busy to do the full works, either cheat (otherwise known as 'buy in') and make it look like your own, or simply simplify. No one will think any more or any less of you, and nobody wants to be greeted by a growling, resentful Princess hostess.

I am sure you have questioned why we even do Friday night dinner, but as Topol from *Fiddler on the Roof* said, 'Tradition! Tradition!'

The Jewish Princess has a long
list of things she has to prepare
in order to be ready for the
Sabbath: manicure, pedicure,
hair colour and cut, facial
and, of course, medication –
I mean, *meditation!*

chopped liver

serves 8

1.3kg onions, roughly chopped
   (you can use frozen
   ready-sliced)
4 tablespoons corn oil
450g ox liver

4 large hard-boiled eggs
   (reserve 1 for decoration)
3 slices brown bread,
   crusts removed
salt and black pepper to taste

Liver is the only meat you buy from a kosher butcher that you need to kosher yourself (with special koshering utensils: ask a kosher butcher for advice). To do this, wash the liver to remove any blood, cover it with coarse salt, broil it on a open flame, then rinse it thoroughly.

In a large frying pan, fry the onions in the corn oil until they turn a dark brown. The browner the onions get without burning, the better the result.

Cut the liver into strips and add it to the fried onions. Cook very slowly until the liver is soft and brown all the way through. Add a little more oil if necessary.

When the onions and liver are fully cooked, add the rest of the ingredients and blend well. Add salt and pepper to taste, but be sure to mix the seasoning thoroughly into the mixture.

Place in a serving dish. Using a coarse (large-holed) grater, grate the reserved egg over the top to decorate, and refrigerate.

If this is not for you, try buying it at your local kosher butcher – but I bet it won't taste half as good as this!

egg and onion

serves 8

10 medium hard-boiled eggs
1 bunch of spring onions,
 finely sliced
olive oil

salt and black pepper to taste
1 avocado (optional)
salad leaves and chopped
 tomatoes, for serving

Using a coarse (large-holed) grater, grate the hard-boiled eggs and stir in the sliced spring onion.

Add enough olive oil to bind the mixture.

Add salt and pepper to taste.

For a different twist, add the avocado: peel it and mash it with a bit of lemon juice and mix it into the egg mixture.

Use an ice-cream scoop to make individual servings. Place each serving on a bed of lettuce leaves and chopped tomatoes.

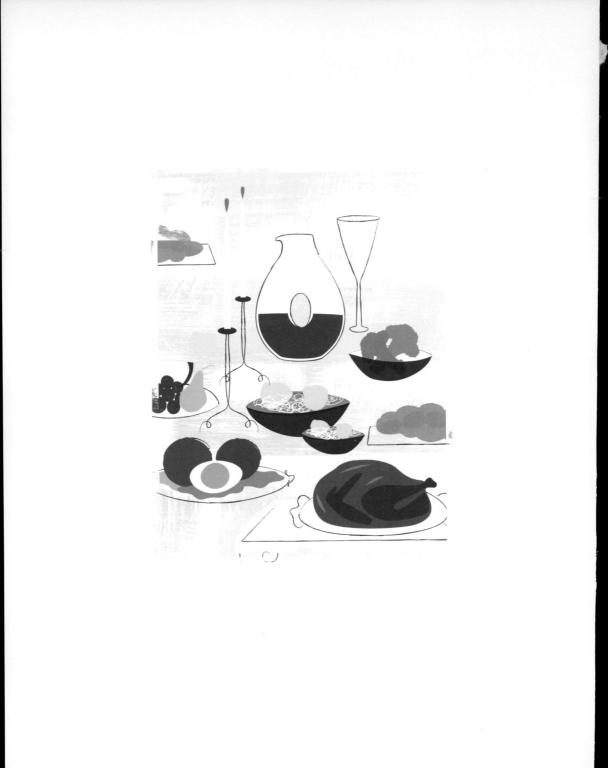

a word about chicken soup

Of all the soups in the Jewish kosher diet, none is more well-known or well-loved than chicken soup. And with good reason: this soup is traditionally served on Friday nights as part of the *Shabbos* dinner, and it is *wonderful*.

Out of all the chicken soups I have ever tasted, however, no two taste the same. Even when a recipe is handed down from mother to daughter, it still does not taste the same.

This is the Mystery and Magic of chicken soup: every recipe has something unique to offer.

I love my own chicken soup because it is full of intense flavour, it is low-fat, and it takes very little time to prepare. In fact, I always make my soup on a Wednesday evening so that I can leave it overnight to cool; this seems to intensify the flavour. Refrigerate it on Thursday morning, then just reheat it for Friday night.

Another handy tip I've discovered concerns *lockshen*: place a heaped tablespoon of cooked *lockshen* into the bottom of each individual soup bowl. As you pour the soup in, the *lockshen* will heat through.

Once you've got used to making chicken soup (whether by following this or any other recipe), you'll probably want to experiment with using other root vegetables or herbs to make your own version of this delicious elixir.

chicken soup

serves 10

1 fowl, skinned and cut
into 8 pieces
NOTE: A fowl is a female
chicken that's a bit like a mother-
in-law – e.g. a 'tough old bird'.
It can be purchased from any
kosher butcher (the fowl, not
the mother-in-law!).
1 bunch of celery hearts, washed
8 carrots, peeled and left whole
4 turnips, peeled and cut into
large chunks

2 parsnips, peeled and cut
into large chunks
1 swede, peeled and cut
into large chunks.
1 large onion, peeled
and cut into large chunks.
2 tablespoons dried parsley
salt and black pepper
to taste
1 tablespoon chicken-flavoured
soup mix to every
600ml water used

Clean the fowl, removing any excess fat and anything else that
looks vaguely suspicious.

Place it in a very large *shissel* (cooking pot).

Add all the rest of the ingredients and cover with cold water.

Bring the soup to the boil. As there is no skin on the fowl,
YOU WILL NOT NEED TO STAND THERE FOR HOURS
REMOVING THE SCUM – so this is a perfect recipe
for Princesses.

Turn the heat down to low, cover the saucepan and leave to
simmer gently for at least five hours, or more. You can test when
the soup is ready by using a fork – the chicken should be so soft
that it should practically fall away from the bone, and the soup
should be a deep golden colour.

to serve
If you have made this in advance, then when you take the soup out of the fridge to serve, get rid of any fat that has risen to the surface by laying several sheets of kitchen paper on top of the soup. When you remove it, the fat will cling to the paper.

If you're not worrying about your carbs, it's traditional to serve this soup with matzo balls and egg noodles (*see* Matzo Balls, page 196). Egg noodles can be purchased in any kosher section of the supermarket or delicatessen, but if you cannot be bothered to *shlep* around, just add some cooked pasta of your choice.

Finally, if you are lucky enough to have the golden eggs (*see* page 81), here's how to cook them. First, wash the eggs and peel off the outer layer. When you're ready to serve your chicken soup, just pop the eggs in the soup (also the matzo balls and *chicklach; see* page 196-7) and bring it to boiling point. Let it boil for five minutes to ensure that the eggs are cooked through.

Ahhhhhhh: Jewish Princess penicillin!

matzo balls (knaidlach)

serves 10

7 large matzos
1 large onion, diced
1 tablespoon olive oil
3 large eggs

3 tablespoons fine matzo meal
1 dessertspoon
  chicken-flavoured seasoning
salt and pepper to taste

Break the matzos into small pieces and place them in a colander. Soak with water. Leave to drain.

Fry the onion in the olive oil until brown.

Place in a mixer the matzos, eggs, matzo meal, onions, chicken flavouring and salt and pepper. Mix all the above until you can see the mixture binding together.

Bring a large saucepan of salted water to the boil.

Wet your hands, then take a teaspoon of the mixture and roll it into a ball.

Continue to make the rest of the balls and then place them in the boiling water for 20 minutes.

This is a great accompaniment to Chicken Soup (see page 194) and is a bit different to the usual knaidlach.

chicklach (kosher-style dim sum)

serves 10

450g minced chicken
2 medium eggs
140g medium matzo meal
6 tablespoons chicken fat
   (use the fat that comes off the
   top of the chicken soup – *see*
   page 194) or dairy-free
   margarine, melted

½ teaspoon cinnamon
½ teaspoon ginger
1 teaspoon dried parsley
Salt and pepper to taste

Mix all the ingredients together and leave the mixture in the fridge to firm up for 20 minutes.

Wet your hands and, using a teaspoon as a measure, form the mixture into small balls.

Fill a large saucepan with salted water and bring it to the boil.

Drop the *chicklach* into the water and simmer for 30 minutes.

Use a slotted spoon to remove the *chicklach* from the water and add them to your chicken soup when needed (*see* below).

This new recipe will become a must as an accompaniment to Chicken Soup (see page 194).

roast chicken

serves 6

1 roasting chicken
2 onions, peeled
black pepper
dried parsley or sage
olive oil

chicken seasoning powder or
   chicken stock powder
12 mushrooms, washed and
   cut into quarters.
spring onions
soy sauce

Preheat the oven to 180°C/350°F/gas mark 4.

Clean the chicken. Just before putting it into the oven, pour boiling water through the centre of the chicken and over the top to make the skin crispy.

Place the chicken in a roasting dish. Place one of the onions inside the chicken's cavity, then season the chicken with black pepper and sprinkle the parsley over the top. Rub a little olive oil into the skin to work the seasoning and parsley into the chicken.

Pour cold water into the bottom of the roasting tin (about 700-850ml depending on the size of chicken) and add a good sprinkling of chicken seasoning or stock powder.

Add the other onion, sliced, and mushrooms, then add the chopped spring onions into the water and a splash of soy sauce onto the chicken.

Cook in the preheated over for one hour 30 minutes. Lovely!

This recipe should serve six, depending on the size of the chicken. Unless my Uncle Michael is one of the guests – then it serves one...

roast potatoes

serves *as many as you like!*

roasting potatoes (allow at least   2-3 tablespoons olive oil
  2 large potatoes per person)   sea salt

Preheat the oven to 180°C/350°F/gas mark 4.

Peel the potatoes and slice them in half.

Take a roasting dish and pour two to three tablespoons of olive oil over the bottom.

On each half of the potatoes, use a sharp knife and make slits (about five) across the potato's width. The slits should be three-quarters of the way down the potato; this allows the olive oil and seasoning to penetrate.

Place the potatoes in the dish, flat-side down.

Sprinkle them with olive oil and sea salt.

Bake in the preheated oven for one and a half hours, turning halfway through.

This elevates the humble roast potato to new heights. Make sure you make plenty for seconds.

shredded red cabbage with apples and sultanas

serves 6

1 red cabbage
1 apple, grated
110g sultanas

5 tablespoons sweetener or sugar
300ml white-wine vinegar
850ml water

Preheat the oven to 150°C/300°F/gas mark 2.

Slice the cabbage into thin shreds and rinse with water.

Mix the cabbage with the apple, sultanas and sweetener and put into an ovenproof dish approximately 30cm square.

Cover the mixture with the vinegar and water, making sure there is enough liquid to cover it completely.

Cover the dish with foil and bake in the preheated oven for approximately three hours. Keep an eye on it, and stir it every half an hour.

Do this the day you're going to have a manicure, as your hands can go a little bit purple. Better still, wear gloves when chopping.

sweet potato and carrot purée

serves 8

4 large sweet potatoes
8 large carrots
1 tablespoon vegetable
  bouillon powder

salt and black pepper to taste
1 tablespoon non-dairy margarine
1 medium egg, beaten

Peel all the vegetables and cut into chunks. Place them all in a large saucepan.

Barely cover the vegetables with water and add the vegetable bouillon powder.

Bring to the boil and simmer for 40 minutes. Drain and then purée.

Preheat the oven to 180°C/350°F/gas mark 4.

Add the seasoning, margarine and egg.

Pour the mixture into an ovenproof dish.

Bake in the preheated oven for 20 minutes.

I always use a hand blender to do the purée; it saves on time and washing up!

apple strudel pie

serves 6

for the dough
450g plain flour
175g caster sugar
225g unsalted butter
   or non-dairy margarine
4 large egg yolks (reserve the
   whites for the filling, below)
2 tablespoons milk
   (or soya milk if you want to
   keep the dessert *parev*)
1 teaspoon baking powder

for the filling
6 apples, peeled and sliced
110g icing sugar
3 teaspoons cinnamon
75g chopped walnuts
2 tablespoons
   vanilla-flavoured sugar
4 large egg whites

Make the dough from all the dough ingredients by using your hands to knead properly on a flat surface until everything is well-combined. If you don't want to get too sticky, mix the ingredients in your food mixer or processor. Cover the egg whites and place them in the fridge for use later.

Wrap 250g of the dough in clingfilm and place it in the freezer for at least an hour, until it is completely frozen and hard.

Wrap the remaining dough in clingfilm and place it in the fridge.

When ready to proceed, preheat the oven to 180°C/350°F/gas mark 4.

Whisk the egg whites until stiff.

Place the rest of the ingredients in a large bowl and stir to make sure there is an even coverage of the sugars and cinnamon.

Roll out the dough from the fridge to whatever thickness works to cover the bottom and sides of the greased ovenproof tin you're using (I always use a 36cm by 20.5cm one).

Place the filling on top and spread the egg whites over the filling. Take out the dough from the freezer and grate it over the egg whites.

Bake for 15 to 20 minutes in the preheated oven, or until the surface is golden and baked through.

If you can't get hold of vanilla sugar, it's easy to make and keep in your store cupboard. Just take two vanilla pods and use a knife to split them down the middle. Cut them into 3cm pieces and fill a small empty spice jar with caster sugar and vanilla. I would wait a week to allow the vanilla to infuse into the sugar. When you are ready to use the sugar, dispose of the vanilla pods.

This is such a delicious dessert that even though your guests may be full, I'm sure they will still indulge in a bissel of strudel pie.

jaffa chocolate mousse

serves 6

225g plain chocolate
  (the 70% cocoa kind)
8 medium eggs, separated

8 teaspoons cointreau
grated orange-flavoured dark
  chocolate, for decoration

Whisk the egg whites until they form stiff peaks.

Melt the chocolate in a double saucepan (bain-marie) on the hob over a gentle heat. If you don't have a double saucepan, use a small bowl placed over a pan of hot water.

When the chocolate has melted, remove it from the heat.

Stir in the egg yolks one at a time.

Using a metal spoon, gently fold in one tablespoon of egg whites, then fold in the rest.

Add the Cointreau and stir gently.

Refrigerate.

Before serving, decorate the mousse with grated orange-flavoured dark chocolate.

lockshen pudding (noodle pudding)

serves 6

250g (1 packet) fine egg
  vermicelli, boiled and rinsed
  with cold water
175g sultanas
2 large eggs
1 dessertspoon cinnamon
1 cooking apple, grated and
  drizzled with lemon juice

3 dessertspoons granulated sugar
1½ teaspoons almond essence
50g non-dairy margarine, melted
2 tablespoons orange cordial

for topping
2 tablespoons sugar
1 teaspoon cinnamon

Preheat the oven to 190°C/375°F/gas mark 5.

Mix all the ingredients, except the sugar and cinnamon for topping, and put the mixture into a greased ovenproof dish.

Mix the sugar together with the cinnamon and sprinkle over the pudding.

Bake in the preheated oven for 45 minutes to one hour.

The Friday night finale.

10

useful information

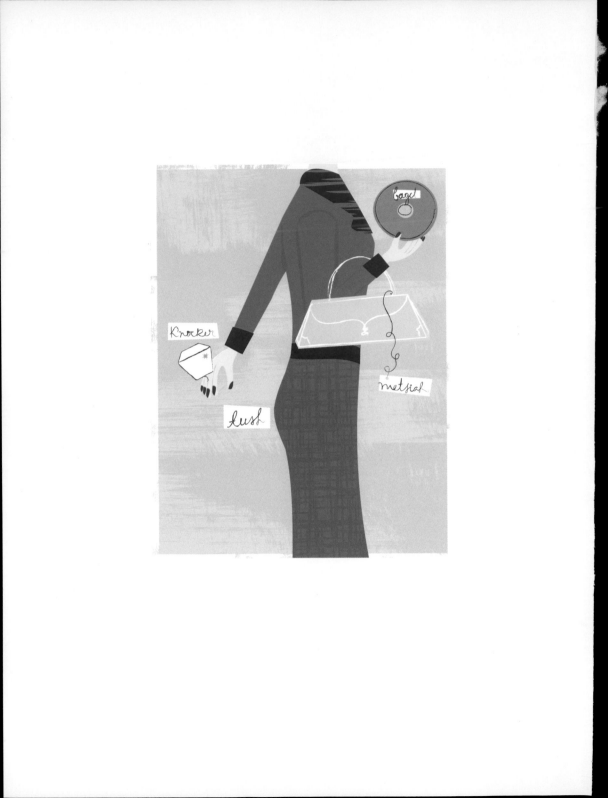

the jewish princess
does yiddish

YID DISH? No, it's not a main course
YID DISH? No, it's not a good-looking Jewish guy!
YIDD-ISH? No, it's not someone who is only a
little bit Jewish.
YID D.I. SH? No, it's not a Jewish detective!

yiddish is a wonderful language

The Yiddish language is like a recipe: take some German and add to it
your Hebrew, season with Slavic, a teaspoon of Romanian and finally,
add a little English and French for that *je ne sais quoi*.

When used, you can express yourself in words that the listener doesn't
have to understand to know exactly what you mean. The words have a
warmth and earthiness to them. They are also incredibly powerful, as one
word will convey feelings that you could not begin to sum up in paragraphs.

Remember *ch* is pronounced as if you are trying to clear your throat.
T at the beginning of a word is silent; for example: *tsures* ('troubles') is
pronounced *sur – es*.

In the following pages I have listed some of my favourite Yiddish
words and expressions, many of which you will find within this book – and
many of which, if you are a Jewish Princess, I am sure you already use.

Please note: because Yiddish comes originally from the Hebrew, and
thus (like Greek) from no English-letter-based alphabet, English spellings
vary from dictionary to dictionary, and even from person to person. Many
Princesses have their own way of spelling, depending on where they
were brought up. Spelling issues aside, I hope you find this useful when
you are looking for just the right word to express how you feel!

yiddish/english glossary

Alter kocker An old person who looks old (obviously). Can't be found in Beverly Hills.

Ashkenazi A Jewish person from central or Eastern Europe.

Bagel Roll with a hole in the middle, eaten a lot on Sundays.

Balabatish An excellent homemaker. A true Jewish Princess!

Bar mitzvah A ceremony marking the religious coming of age of a 13-year-old boy (very expensive party).

Bashayrt Fate.

Bat mitzvah Ceremony marking the religious coming of age of a 12-year-old girl (also very expensive!).

Bissel A very small amount.

Blintz Pancake filled with cream cheese (*see* page 132).

Borscht Beetroot soup (*see* page 63).

Borscht Belt Popular holiday resort in the Catskill Mountains in upper New York State. For the European version, go to Grand Rimini in Italy.

Boychik Young boy.

Bris Circumcision for baby boys (ouch!).

Brocheh Blessing. There is a different one for every situation.

Broyges An argument with bad feeling. Happens a lot with families.

Bubbeleh Term of endearment – or a Passover pancake.

Bubbeh Grandmother (always imagine an old-looking grandma – not a surgically enhanced Silver Surfer!).

Bubbeh-myseh Made-up story. I know some people – and they are all under 12 – who are very good at these!

Bupkes Nothing.

Challah Platted loaf used mainly for the Sabbath meal, delicious (*see* page 134 for Choca-Challa Pudding).

Challish To want something, as in 'I *challish* for it.'

Chanukah The Festival of Lights (normally falls near Christmas). Eight days of presents: a JP's favourite time of the year!

Chasid Member of an orthodox religious sect.

Chayshik (pronounced *hay – shik*) Enthusiasm.

Chazzen Singer in Synagogue (like Neil Diamond in *The Jazz Singer* if you're lucky).

Chazzer Being greedy.

Cheder A school where children learn about the Jewish religion.

Chochem A clever person.

Cholent Meat stew that is cooked overnight (*see* page 96).

Chotchkeh Knick-knack.

Chrayn Horseradish sauce. Delicious hot red sauce that accompanies fish.

Chuppah Wedding canopy.

Chutzpah Cheek or nerve. A Jewish Princess has plenty of this!

Diaspora The historical dispersion of the Jews.
Doven Pray.
Drek A vulgar expression for ugly.

Farfel Tiny noodles.
Faygeleh Homosexual.
Feh! Ugh! Used when you don't like something.
Ferbissener A bitter person.
Fershtinkiner Revolting and smelly.
Flayshedik Kosher meat dishes.
Fliegel Chicken wing.
Forspeise A taster or appetizer.
Fress Eat a lot.
Frum Religious person.
Frummer Religious person.

Gatkes Long johns.
Gedempte Slowly cooked.
Gefilte fish A dish made from chopped fish; it can be fried or boiled.
Gelt Money.
Gesundheit You say it when someone sneezes and it means health.
Get A Jewish divorce.
Gavalt Shock. People usually say *Oy gavalt!* if something really bad happens.
Glatt kosher Strictly kosher.
Glitch When something goes wrong.
Golem Artificially created man.
Gonif A thief.
Gornisht Nothing.

Haggadah A book telling the Passover story.
Haimish (No, not a Scotsman...) Friendly and warm.
Halachah Religious law.

Halva Sweets made from sesame seeds (*see* page 138 for Honey Halva Ice Cream).
Hatikvah Israeli national anthem.

Kaddish Mourner's prayer.
Kapel or *Kippot* Skullcap Jewish men wear in synagogue – and if religious they wear all the time.
Kashrus Dietary laws.
Kibbutz Israeli cooperative agricultural settlement.
Kichel A biscuit.
Kiddush Blessing recited over wine or bread on the Sabbath or at a festival.
Kinder Children.
Kishkes Guts.
Klutz Clumsy person.
Knaidlach Matzo balls (*see* page 196).
Knish Baked roll filled with potato or meat.
K'nocker A big shot. Or a big diamond.
Krank Something annoying.
Kreplach Ravioli with chopped meat.
Kugel Noodle or potato pudding.
Kvell To glow with pride.
Kvetch To complain.

Langer Lockshen Tall person, very thin – spaghetti-like.
Latke Potato pancake.
Lechayim A toast to life.
Levoyah Funeral.
Loch in kop A hole in the head.
Lockshen Noodles.
Lox Smoked salmon.
Lubavitch A religious sect of orthodox Jews.
Macher An organizer.

Machetunim Relatives by marriage.
Matzo Unleavened bread.
Matzo-brie Matzo mixed with egg to make an omelette.
Mazel Good luck.
Mazel tov Congratulations.
Megillah A long story. It derives from the story of Esther at Purim.
Menorah Candelabra lit at Chanukah.
Mentsh A good person.
Meshugga Mad.
Meshuggener A mad person.
Metsiah A bargain – like getting a Gucci handbag at 70 percent off!
Mezuzah Religious scroll in an encasement attached to a door.
Mieskayt An ugly person.
Mikvah A ritual bath.
Milchik Dairy foods.
Minyan Ten men required for religious services.
Mishegass A mad idea.
Mitzvah A good idea.
Mockers Put bad luck on something.
Mogen Dovid A Star of David.
Mohel The man who performs the circumcision (ouch!).
Momzer Bastard.

Naches Pride from your children (*Shlepping naches* from the *kinder*).
Nebbish Nerdy person.
Noodge To nudge/remind.
Nosh Snacking: something I love to do!
Noo So?
Nudnik An annoying person.

Over sholom Passed away.
Oy! An exclamation of surprise.

Oy veh! An exclamation of shock.
Parev Foods that contain no dairy products.
Pesach Passover.
Pish To urinate.
Pletzel Like a bagel without the hole and with poppy seeds and onion on top.
Polkeh Chicken drumstick.
Puppik Navel.
Putz Idiot.

Rachmones Pity.
Rebbe Rabbi.
Rebbitsen Rabbi's wife.
Rosh Hashana The Jewish New Year.

Saychel Common sense; using your head.
Seder The meal we eat first and second night of Passover.
Sefer Torah The scroll containing the five Books of Moses.
Sephadi A Jewish person from Spanish or Portuguese descent.
Shabbos The Sabbath.
Shadchen A matchmaker.
Shah Shut up!
Sha'koyach Congratulations.
Shamus No, not an Irish person – a detective.
Shayn Pretty.
Sheitel A wig worn by a married Orthodox woman.
Shiddach A possible marriage introduction.
Shiker Drunk.
Shissel A cooking pot.
Shivah A seven-day period of mourning.

Shlemiel An idiot.

Shlep To carry or to go a long way.

Shlepper Someone who carries all your heavy goods.

Shloch An untidy person.

Shlong The male organ (large).

Shluff To have a sleep.

Shmaltz Chicken fat. Or being too sentimental (no, I don't know why, either).

Shmatta Rags, cheap clothes. Can be said sarcastically when you are wearing your brand-new D&G.

Shmear To spread ('A *shmear* of cream cheese on my bagel, please.') Or to bribe.

Shmendrick An idiot.

Shmo An idiot.

Shmooze To coax with charming behaviour (JP's are very good at this).

Shmuck An idiot. Or a penis...

Shmutzy Looking unkempt or dirty.

Shnide To do something underhanded.

Shnorrer A mean person.

Shochet The ritual slaughter of animals for kosher meat.

Shofar A ram's horn blown in synagogues on the new year.

Sholom Peace.

Shpilkes When you are restless.

Shpritz A spray or squirt of something.

Shtetl A Jewish village in Eastern Europe.

Shtick Something that is funny.

Shtook In trouble.

Shtoom! Keep quiet! Can be said to children when noisy or when you want to keep something quiet.

Shtup A vulgar word for sexual intercourse; it also means tipped.

Shul Synagogue

Shvitz To be hot.

Shyster A thief or unscrupulous person.

Siddur A prayer book.

Simcha A joyous occasion. A common expression is 'Only on *simchas*'.

Smetana A type of sour cream.

Spiel A salesman's chat when he's talking to a client.

Tallis A Jewish prayer shawl (not a pashmina...).

Talmud Jewish law and tradition.

Tush Bottom.

Torah The Five Books of Moses.

Treif See page 18. Un-kosher – prawns, pork, etc.

Tsedrayt A mad person.

Tsures Troubles.

Tzaddik A righteous man.

Tzimmes (*see* page 98) A dish of cooked meat and vegetables, and sometimes with fruit.

Worsht (pronounced *vorsht*) Salami.

Yachna A gossip.

Yahrtzeit The anniversary of a death.

Yamulka Skullcap – same as *kapel*.

Yenta A female gossip.

Yiches Prestige.

Yiddishe Jewish.

Yiddishkeit Jewishness.

Yom kippur The Day of Attonement.

Yom tov A Jewish holiday.

Zaydeh Grandfather.

Zey gezunt Go in good health.

princess pointers

Every Princess knows that a little bit of advice can be invaluable (except when it comes from your mother-in-law). In the kitchen, having a few tips up your sleeve not only makes life easier, but it can also cut down on time, stop your hands smelling of onions and – most importantly – impress your mother-in-law. So here are a few that I find most handy.

1   If you place some kitchen paper folded double on top of your chicken soup, then lift it off, all the fat comes away with it.

2   If you're looking for *challah*, matzo meal, chicken-soup mix, dairy-free creamer or dairy-free margarine, just try your local kosher deli or the kosher section at your supermarket. Or better still, have a look at our website (*see* page 221).

3   When cutting fresh bread and cakes, first dip your knife in boiling water. You will get a lovely, clean slice.

4   A glass will not crack or break if you place a spoon in it first before pouring in hot liquid (Science Teacher, a.k.a. son aged 12, taught me that one).

5   When presenting food or arranging your flowers, always use odd numbers.

6   Prick sausages with a fork before cooking, as this prevents them from bursting.

7   When slicing an onion, don your rubber gloves to avoid smelly hands. Let the water run to avoid sliding mascara – or better still, buy frozen ready-sliced onions.

8   If your soup or stew is too salty, add a teaspoonful of sugar or a little grated raw potato and cook gently for a few minutes.

9   When chopping herbs, use a pair of kitchen scissors.

10   When peeling hard-boiled eggs, immerse them in cold water, then roll on kitchen paper to remove the shells.

11   If a guest offers to bring a dish, say 'YES!'

12   Always check your store cupboard for ingredients before baking.

13   Always, always turn the oven on *before* you start making a cake in order that it will reach the correct temperature.

14   Double up! If you're going to the trouble of making a cake, why not make two and freeze one? Then you're always prepared for those surprise guests.

15   Get the kids involved. This has many benefits. Firstly, it turns them on to cooking (future Princes and Princesses). Secondly, it makes them more adventurous when it comes to eating. Thirdly, they will be able to cook for you in your old age.

16   If you have great help, hang on to her (or even *him*). Don't forget to offer praise for doing a great job.

17   Always wash your hands before cooking, and after you have handled raw meat and eggs.

18   When using eggs, always crack them into a glass bowl one at a time, before adding them to any other ingredients. This helps avoid the shell going into the mixture, and you can also see if any are bad (or unkosher, if they contain blood spots).

19   Insert a sharp blade into a cake to see if it's done. If it comes out clean, your cake has baked.

20 To enable a cake to come out of the tin easily, make sure you grease (with butter) and flour it before pouring in the mixture – regardless of whether or not the recipe calls for it.

21 When removing a cake from a loose-bottomed tin, place the tin on a tin can and press down to lift off the sides.

22 Don't forget to use icing sugar – it's like fairy dust. Sprinkle over cakes and fruit for that little extra touch.

23 When using a loose-bottomed tin, wrap aluminium foil around the bottom to prevent the mixture from seeping out. This prevents your oven from getting dirty.

24 When you are at the checkout, don't be afraid to ask for a packer – or better still, shop online.

25 Check your sell-by dates. After all, you won't want to poison your family – so if in doubt, chuck it out.

26 Know your oven like a friend. They all vary, and some cook quicker than others, so keep this in mind when following recipes.

27 Don't forget: if you spend a long time in the car (and most JPs do this) always have water, tissues, coins for meters, Junior JP snacks, hand cream and paracetamol to hand.

28 When buying aluminium foil, baking parchment and cling film, always buy the jumbo size.

29 Wear your Jewish Princess apron when cooking to protect those couture creations.

30 Always wear your Jewish Princess oven gloves to protect your perfect manicure.

the jewish princess parting note

The Jewish Princess loves to party, but you don't need to go to a party in order to *parteee!* Every day can be a party. It's just how you decide to live your life.

Find your inner Princess and you will see that the little things in life – like eating with your friends and family, sitting down and having a nice cup of tea, laughing on the phone at some amusing tale, or treating yourself to a little something (I find handbags always cheer me up enormously); in other words, finding the things that make you happy (and often this means *making others* happy) – will show you that the Jewish Princess Champagne Theory is true.

'What's the Jewish Princess Champagne Theory?' I hear you ask.

Well, here it is:

'Is the Champagne Bottle of Life half-full or half-empty?'

For every Jewish Princess, the answer is: 'The Champagne Bottle of Life is ALWAYS half-full.'

But of course, she always orders another bottle to keep in reserve. (She can't help it. It's genetic.)

I know that the pace of this hectic world can sometimes make you feel like you're riding on a very fast train and hanging on for dear life; well, hang on in there, because eventually you *will* get to your destination. If you just try and arrive in style, however, no one will ever be the wiser.

Anyway, enough of Princess Philosophy.

What I really want to say is GOODBYE until the next time we meet, which I am sure will be very soon, as we live in a very small world. Of course, being a Jewish Princess I hate to say goodbye; I prefer to say *sholom.*

Peace to all my Princess People, whether you are Jewish, Christian, Catholic, Hindu, Muslim, Atheist... Let's try and find our common ground, so that we can come together and share our cultures and our recipes.

Let us sit down for dinner sometime and enjoy the simple things in life (like Bvlgari jewellery).

Now I really must go – I have a very important meeting. Yes, you guessed it: HAIRDRESSER!

I may be gone for a while, as I need my colour doing, so while I'm away, just remember the Three Ps:

* positive
* productive

And, of course:

* princesslike!

XXXXXXXXXX

if all else fails…

…call the caterer!